"There is a considerable amount of research concerning leadership and its different aspects in academic and organizational settings. Frequently it focuses on characteristics of influential leaders or their communication style, but not much emphasis has been put on the topic of narcissistic leadership. This book focuses entirely on this phenomenon, and I find it not only well-written and reader-friendly but especially useful for students and managers interested in exploring this angle of leadership. I highly recommend it."

Judit Olah, *University of Debrecen*

"Despite the seemingly remarkable progress in presenting narcissism in an organizational framework and leadership role, the perception of narcissistic leaders based on the leader evaluation method is omitted. This book exquisitely bridges this gap and provides valuable insights on the topic of narcissistic leadership."

Magdalena Stuss, *Jagiellonian University*

Leadership and Narcissism in the Organization

Narcissists are seen as people who could inspire others due to their strong charisma, great vision, and ability to convince the crowd that they possess features that others don't. They have followers and fans, and the ability to control them. On the other hand, narcissistic leaders express a lack of empathy and high levels of aggression and show constant criticism of others while refusing feedback on their performance. Those features indicate that such leaders have a strong sense of entitlement of superiority; therefore, it is hard to work with them. In the corporate world, many individuals with narcissistic personalities are chosen as leaders of organizations or teams, which often harms their co-workers and subordinates. Very few lower-level employees have a positive perception of their narcissistic leaders or are satisfied with their job, and so there is need to measure through qualitative research based on already existing articles in a given subject the correlation between the perception of narcissistic leader and the leader evaluation method.

This book gives insight into psychology and management by linking the narcissistic personality with the leadership role and with the method of evaluating a leader, along with discussing the positive or negative outcomes of their leadership. Readers will learn about the phenomenon of narcissistic individuals and leaders as well as the attributes and traits of such a person. This research monograph will be of interest to researchers, academics, and advanced students in the fields of work and organizational psychology and leadership studies.

Mateusz Grzesiak is an Assistant Professor at the Department of Management of the WSB University, Poland. He holds a Ph.D. in management, Ph.D. in education, and Psy.D. in psychology.

Routledge Studies in Leadership Research

21 **Adaptive Leadership in a Global Economy**
Perspective for Application and Scholarship
Edited by Mohammed Raei and Harriette Thurber Rasmussen

22 **Women Business Leaders**
Identity, Resistance, and Alternative Forms of Knowledge in Saudi Arabia
Liela A. Jamjoom

23 **Responsible Leadership in Corporate Governance**
An Integrative Approach
Monique Cikaliuk, Ljiljana Eraković, Brad Jackson, Chris Noonan and Susan Watson

24 **Leadership and China**
Philosophy, Place and Practice
Edited by Ralph J Bathurst and Michelle Sitong Chen

25 **Leadership and Narcissism in the Organization**
Mateusz Grzesiak

26 **Public Sector Leadership**
A Human-Centred Approach
Petri Virtanen, Marika Tammeaid and Harri Jalonen

27 **Toxic Leadership**
Research and Cases
Steven Walker and Daryl Watkins

For more information about this series please visit: https://www.routledge.com/Routledge-Studies-in-Leadership-Research/book-series/RSLR

Leadership and Narcissism in the Organization

Mateusz Grzesiak

Routledge
Taylor & Francis Group
NEW YORK AND LONDON

First published 2023
by Routledge
605 Third Avenue, New York, NY 10158

and by Routledge
4 Park Square, Milton Park, Abingdon, Oxon, OX14 4RN

Routledge is an imprint of the Taylor & Francis Group, an informa business

Library of Congress Cataloging-in-Publication Data
Names: Grzesiak, Mateusz, author.
Title: Leadership and narcissism in the organization / Mateusz Grzesiak.
Description: 1 Edition. | New York, NY: Routledge, 2023. |
Series: Routledge studies in leadership research |
Includes bibliographical references and index.
Identifiers: LCCN 2022023998 | ISBN 9781032197388 (hardback) |
ISBN 9781032197449 (paperback) | ISBN 9781003260646 (ebook)
Subjects: LCSH: Leadership—Psychological aspects. |
Narcissism. | Psychology, Industrial.
Classification: LCC HD57.7 .G79 2023 |
DDC 658.4/092—dc23/eng/20220808
LC record available at https://lccn.loc.gov/2022023998

The project is funded under the program of the Minister of Education and Science titled "Regional Initiative of Excellence" in 2019–2022, project number 018/RID/2018/19, the amount of funding PLN 10 788 423,16.

ISBN: 978-1-032-19738-8 (hbk)
ISBN: 978-1-032-19744-9 (pbk)
ISBN: 978-1-003-26064-6 (ebk)

DOI: 10.4324/9781003260646

Typeset in Bembo
by codeMantra

Contents

1 Narcissism and Leadership

An Overview

There is a socio-economic interest in people with narcissistic personality traits and the traits' correlation with the leadership position that many of them hold (Braun, 2017). Narcissism is present in all aspects of people's lives and usually starts to manifest itself in younger adults. Such individuals are described as the "Me" generation; thus, "they have highly inflated, unrealistically positive views of the self" in which the entire world revolves around them (Foster, Campbell, & Twenge, 2003, p. 1). Social media and the advancement of electronic technology that allow people to access the internet, and therefore, the whole world allow these individuals to express themselves and promote their narcissistic behaviors (Biolcati & Passini, 2018). Social media such as Facebook, Twitter, or Instagram incentivize taking selfies and posting "Instagram stories" about their personal life and everyday events (Gnambs & Appel, 2017). The same behavior is also transferred to work settings, where individuals with narcissistic traits hold management and leadership positions.

Narcissism is characterized by positive but also dark personality traits. Narcissists are energetic and charismatic; therefore, they reach significant heights in their careers in organizations. However, when they reach a certain level of promotion, they start to show their turbulent side, which has drastic consequences for the leader-follower level (Blair, Helland, & Walton, 2017). The leader-follower interaction may have various outcomes that highly reflect the work of both parties. A narcissistic leader's perception plays a crucial role in the leader-follower relationship (Nevicka et al., 2018). The different perceptions of a narcissistic leader in the organization can be seen by the disparities between the leader's self-evaluation and other people's reports on the leader (Mainah & Perkins, 2016). The self-report, or the narcissistic leader's self-evaluation, is always positive and portrays the narcissist leader in a bright light (Braun, 2017). However, when other people write down their perceptions of the narcissistic leader, the description changes dramatically (Korhonen, 2017). The key reason for this is that followers are always more critical of their supervisors, which may stem from the leaders' dominant and abusive behavior (Schilling & Schyns, 2012).

The topic of a narcissistic leader has recently gained popularity, especially since there has been an increase of individuals with narcissistic

DOI: 10.4324/9781003260646-1

personalities who reach leadership positions in organizations. It is worth examining the impact of narcissistic leaders on their subordinates through the leader evaluation lens. The chapter uses a systematic literature review to identify the various types of assessment of a narcissistic leader in an organization and their influence on the leader-follower outcomes. The study aimed to argue that a narcissistic leader's perception varies depending on the leader's evaluation. The chapter also discusses the effect that the perception of a narcissistic leader has on their followers at work.

Background of the Problem

In the times of "Generation Me," there are a significant number of individuals who put their needs in front of everybody else's for everything they do (Gnambs & Appel, 2017). Most people believe this is a very selfish approach to life and disregard such behavior (Foster, Campbell, & Twenge, 2003). Narcissistic people are very confident, bring themselves up, and show others that they believe they are superior. Being narcissistic is beneficial but can also be very problematic. There is a fine line between the two aspects of this personality trait, and it is easy to cross it and become a selfish and ignorant person.

Narcissistic leaders have been of much value to their employers because of their attributes. Features such as enthusiasm, vision, charisma, sense of humor, and charm are beneficial because they can contribute to the organization's growth and can make it look much nicer in the eyes of the clients and competitors (Nevicka et al., 2018). Although company owners and CEOs may find these features desirable, they hurt junior-level employees. The arrogance and selfishness of narcissistic leaders can wear people down, make them less productive at work, and, in some cases, provoke them to change their jobs, which may lead to high employee turnover (Braun, 2017). This phenomenon has been present almost worldwide, especially in individualistic cultures, where narcissistic individuals and leaders more frequently emerge. This study attempted to show that junior-level employees, immediate coworkers, and subordinates of a narcissistic leader have a negative perception of these leaders, which is why often these groups express negative behaviors toward work and their supervisors. The second purpose of the study was to present CEOs with information on why it is not always the best idea to hire narcissistic persons as leaders at any company level because it might affect other employees' work.

Statement of the Problem

Recent research has examined narcissism in the context of an organizational framework and leadership role within an organization (Baars, 2015; Braun, 2017; Grijalva et al., 2014; Nevicka et al., 2018). Hart et al. (2017)

and Mainah and Perkins (2016) have outlined the scope of the problem and the different types of narcissism noticeable in the company settings. The authors have shown that grandiose narcissism is related to having a favorable opinion of oneself, whereas vulnerable narcissism is associated with fear of negative perception. Researchers have also outlined the positive and negative features of narcissistic leaders (Grijalva et al., 2014; Hart et al., 2017; Nevicka et al., 2018). Some have focused on the negative aspects of narcissistic personalities (Galvin, Lange, & Ashforth, 2014; Korhonen, 2017; Mainah & Perkins, 2016) while others have examined the positive aspects of a narcissistic leader. The relevant literature has also presented the problem using the perspective of evaluation forms and of the type of participants included in the assessment of narcissistic leaders (Galvin, Lange, & Ashforth, 2014; Grijalva et al., 2014; Hart et al., 2017; Nevicka et al., 2018; Schilling & Schyns, 2012). This literature indicates that leaders are assessed either through self-reporting or reporting by followers or significant others, which influences how the narcissistic leader is perceived in the company setting. The existing research has only provided general information on this subject. The primary aim that this study pursued is to test how the different types of independent variables, such as self-evaluation and evaluation by others of narcissistic leaders, influence the perception of narcissistic leaders in an organization. The secondary issue was to examine the impact the opinion of a narcissistic leader has on an organization's outcome and employee well-being.

Purpose of the Study

The research was based on a qualitative systematic review of archival data on narcissism, narcissistic personality traits, narcissistic leaders, the perception of narcissism, and forms of evaluation of narcissistic leaders in organizations. This was done to examine how the various types of assessments of narcissistic leaders affect the perception of a narcissistic leader in an organization and the employees' well-being. This research method was the most appropriate for the proposed topic because many researchers have already examined a similar problem, and, therefore, data on this subject already exist. The research was based on these findings and extended the topic to show that such leaders' perception has been linked with the form of evaluation, which impacts the outcomes of such behavior by negatively affecting other employees, especially lower-level ones. This research method also showed that such leaders' narcissistic behavior has a very negative influence on employees of a given organization, causing stress and lack of job motivation, lowering effectiveness and job satisfaction, and in some cases, causing employees to resign from work. Thus, the literature review went in three directions to answer the following questions.

First, it examined the forms of evaluation of narcissistic leaders in organizations. Various types of employee assessments have been used in companies such as questionnaires, either online or, in the traditional manner, on paper (Braun et al., 2016; Nevicka et al., 2011). However, the most valuable evaluation aspect includes the supervisor report, subordinate report, and peer report of the narcissistic leader (Cullen, Gentry, & Yammarino, 2015; Grijalva et al., 2014). Second, the literature review discussed the impact each type of employee evaluation had on the narcissistic leader's perception. The study explained that when a narcissistic leader's supervisors, subordinates, or peers evaluated the leader, often they perceived the leader in a negative light (Cullen, Gentry, & Yammarino, 2015; Nevicka et al., 2018). However, when a narcissistic leader performed a self-evaluation, his ideation about himself as a leader was always presented in good light (Keller Hansbrough & Jones, 2014; Meurs et al., 2013). Third, the literature has also tested whether the leader's perception impacted their relationship with their subordinates and whether this impact was positive or negative. The gathered research has argued that the high self-assessment that narcissistic leaders have caused disagreements and conflicts between them and their subordinates, who somehow threaten their superiors' ego (Nevicka, Hartog, & De Hoogh, 2016).

Research Questions

RQ1. What were the various methods of narcissistic leader evaluation used to assess leaders in an organization?

RQ2. What impact various forms of narcissistic leader evaluation had on how the leaders of an organization were perceived (whether positively or negatively)?

RQ3. What influence the narcissistic leader had on their subordinates, and what was the outcome of this influence?

Theoretical Framework

To begin with the theoretical framework, the problem that was examined in the given research concerned how a narcissistic leader is perceived in their organization, considering various evaluation forms of such a leader. The next aspect of this research chapter was analyzing the impact that the perception of a narcissistic leader had on the employees' outcomes. It is quite apparent that there has recently been a rise in narcissistic tendencies. To understand this issue, it is essential to explain the origin, development, and theory of narcissism. The next section discusses narcissism in leadership and how subordinates and leaders perceive the narcissistic leader. The foundation for the presented research was the theories of narcissistic leaders.

This research has thus used the theory on the origin of narcissism as presented by Braun (2017), the definition from the Diagnostic and Statistical Manual of Mental Disorders (DSM-5), and work performed by Nevicka et al. (2018). It has explained the overall overview of the main features of a narcissistic personality. The next theory included in the dissertation expressed by Nevicka et al. (2018), Keller Hansbrough & Jones (2014), Baars (2015), and other researchers has linked the narcissistic personality with a leadership role, presenting the good and bad personality traits of narcissistic leaders. Third, the research has presented various evaluation forms of a narcissistic leader in the organization and how they impact the perception others have of narcissistic leaders. The last component of the dissertation was a review of how the opinion of a narcissistic leader (good or bad) and the leader's actions influence the leader's subordinates and coworkers. Therefore, the main questions arose: What are the forms of leader evaluations in organizations? What is the perception of a narcissistic leader in an organization? Is it negative or positive? What impact does it have on leader-follower relations?

The first theories concerning narcissism were presented by Braun (2017). The author stated that narcissism first appeared in Greek mythology, where a young boy named Narcissus fell in love with his reflection. Amazed by his beauty, the boy tried to seduce his reflection. The DSM-5's (American Psychiatric Association, 2013) current definition of narcissism is that it is a personality disorder. Narcissistic personality disorder (NPD) contains the following features: "arrogance, power, entitlement, brilliance, beauty, attention-seeking, lack of empathy, grandiosity, and depression," and many others (Morey & Stanger, 2012). Narcissism has also been examined in the context of leadership in all types of organizations.

A narcissistic individual's personality traits have been viewed as one of the primary features of a future leader. Nevicka et al. (2018) created a psychological portrait of such a leader, which consists of charisma, enthusiasm, attractive vision, personal charm, and humor. In their work, Owens, Wallace, and Waldman (2015) added that a good leader should also be able to take risks and be persistent in achieving their goals. The other crucial aspect of this dissertation was analyzing various evaluation forms of leaders within the organization that can show how leaders are perceived within a given organization. Braun (2017) divided this evaluation into two categories: the self-evaluation and the "others-report." The self-evaluation is often completed by the narcissistic leader, whereas the others' assessment is conducted by other employees such as subordinates, coworkers, or followers. It has been the primary variable that impacted the perception of a narcissistic leader. The positive opinion of a leader is associated with the favorable traits of narcissistic personalities such as charisma, charm, grand vision, innovativeness, persistent pursuit of goals, and risk-taking (Keller et al., 2014; Nevicka et al., 2013; Owens, Wallace, & Waldman, 2015). However, it has also been pointed out by researchers that narcissistic leaders have been viewed in a negative light, which happens when they expressed the following features: arrogance, dominance, selfishness (Nevicka et al., 2013), admiration-seeking, despotism (Hua-Qiang, Guang-Lei, & Zhi-Hui, 2018), public ridiculing, taking credit for others' work, and hostility (Keller Hansbrough & Jones, 2014).

The research's primary purpose was to argue that the assessment methods of narcissistic leaders play a crucial role in the perception of a narcissistic leader in the organization. Researchers have shown that it is desirable for future leaders to have narcissistic personality traits. Thus, such people should have the strengths and charisma to pursue their careers and lead the company to significant heights on the market. The research has discussed where narcissism comes from and provided a definition of it to present an overview of the main features of a narcissistic personality. The narcissistic personality has been linked with a leadership role as well as the forms of evaluation of such leaders. The study's purpose was to show that the type of leaders' assessment impacts a narcissistic leader's perception in the organization, the positive and negative impression. How does the opinion of a narcissistic leader in an organization influence the well-being of employees? The research itself was based on an article review of already-existing data on narcissism, narcissistic personality traits, narcissistic leaders, the perception of narcissism, and the evaluation of narcissistic leaders in the organization. The study aimed to show that after performing employee evaluations of narcissistic leaders in the organization, such a leader was perceived negatively by their subordinates. The stress related to this perception then severely impacts their well-being and work effectiveness.

Significance of the Study

The concept of a narcissistic leader in an organization has been examined by researchers who discussed many aspects of this topic. The issue is broad because, although narcissistic individuals have features that make them great leaders, they also have characteristics that push people away or have an adverse influence on employees. This means that other people working in a given organization may have various opinions of a specific narcissistic leader. Therefore, this study was focused on presenting the aspect of the narcissistic individual as a leader in an organization and the perception of such a leader by other employees. The gathered literature has shown that companies have used various forms of employee assessments, which were a core element of this study. This perception of a narcissistic leader in an organization has often depended on how and by whom the narcissistic leader was evaluated (Braun, 2017). The research has examined the correlation between the evaluation of narcissistic leaders in organizations and their perception. It has measured how the opinion of such a leader changed if they were assessed by their subordinates, coworkers, or through self-evaluation. The study presented that the narcissistic leader's perception depends on the form of evaluation and that it may have the opposite outcome concerning it.

This study's importance stems from the fact that society worldwide has changed and people more frequently display narcissistic personality traits such as having self-focus, favoring material goods, having feelings of entitlement, and many others (Foster, Campbell, & Twenge, 2003). The literature has also shown that people who have narcissistic personality traits, such as charisma and great vision, are highly desired as leaders, managers, and directors of organizations (Nevicka et al., 2018). It has also been noted that such individuals are indeed chosen as high-level managers and leaders, as their traits prove to be favorable for business. Nevertheless, working with such individuals may have a destructive influence on close subordinates. This is because these leaders are often very demanding and aggressive, put their well-being over the good of their employees, exaggerate, or take credit for successes as if they were the sole reason for them. The last part of the chapter examines the influence of the narcissistic individual on their subordinates or followers as it correlates to the narcissistic leader's perception.

The research information has broadened the existing study on this topic of narcissistic leaders in the organization by verifying various forms of narcissistic leader evaluation and presenting the opinion that the leaders and their subordinates have about such persona in correlation with it. This information has been of excellent value for business owners and directors of all sorts of organizations. It has given them an overview of how other employees might perceive leaders with narcissistic personality traits. Such knowledge could be crucial for balancing the need for a narcissistic but charismatic and effective leader and other employees' effectiveness and happiness.

Limitations and Delimitations of the Study

The research was based on the review of already-existing articles from online databases; these articles were extracted from psychological, economic, and managerial scholarly journals. The materials were selected using strict criteria. The first step was to search the EBSCO host's online database for the keywords associated with the organization's narcissistic leader. Such terms included words such as "narcissism," "narcissistic leaders," "employee," "follower," "perception of a narcissistic leader," "narcissistic CEO," and many variations of these words. The search resulted in 350 articles on the presented subject from 1914 to 2019, which followed specific criteria divided into three groups. One group consisted of research articles containing information about a narcissistic leader's perception (positive and negative). The other group included articles that provided information on the forms of evaluations of narcissistic leaders such as self-reports and others' reports. The third group contained articles with information about the outcome that a narcissistic leader's behavior had on employees, focusing on the negative impacts of these leaders.

The first criterion was the materials containing few forms of leader evaluation with the main focus on the leader's self-evaluation and the evaluations by others (the followers' assessment; Galvin, Lange, & Ashforth, 2014; Grijalva et al., 2014; Hart et al., 2017; Nevicka et al., 2018; Schilling & Schyns, 2012). The following research has indicated that in the company setting, the leaders' assessment has either been performed through self-reporting or other-reporting done by followers or any other significant actors associated with the leaders, which influenced the narcissistic leader's perception.

The second criterion for the investigation included articles that contain data on how narcissistic leaders are viewed in the organization, encompassing both positive and negative opinions (Baars, 2015; Braun, 2017; Grijalva et al., 2014; Nevicka et al., 2018). It has been noted through all reviewed articles the quantitative measures to assess the narcissism of leaders.

The other set of criteria included articles containing information on the impact of narcissistic leader behavior on the well-being of employees and the organization (Galvin, Lange, & Ashforth, 2014; Grijalva et al., 2014; Hart et al., 2017; Nevicka et al., 2018; Mainah & Perkins, 2016; Schilling & Schyns, 2012). This criterion was necessary as the purpose of the review was to describe relationships between narcissistic leaders and organizational outcomes.

The main limitation of this study concerned the articles chosen for the research. The publications selected for review did not include a psychoanalytical perspective of this phenomenon. This problem was only mentioned in the overall explanation of the personality traits of a narcissistic individual. The second limitation was that the articles used in the study were those found through the EBSCO host search engine, available from the California Southern University, which limited the number of publications that were available to only those on this site. The articles which were not peer-reviewed and not published in scholarly journals were also omitted. Furthermore, the publications were selected only if they included the two forms of narcissistic leaders' assessment: self-assessment and assessments by others. This limited the number of articles used for the study. This research's following limitation was eliminating other study designs such as computer simulation, field surveys, lab experiments, and case studies.

The following limitation of the research stemmed from set criteria limiting the participants of the study. The conducted research only measured narcissism among leaders while omitting the other two so-called dark traits, Machiavellianism and psychopathy. There was also a visible generalization of followers that excluded their personality traits and the impact that those traits can have on the perception of narcissistic leaders. Lastly, this research neglected to measure the opinion of narcissistic leaders on the team level, which measures the connection between the leader and their coworkers. Further research should be performed on this subject to measure how narcissistic leaders' perceptions have changed over time.

Definitions and Key Terms

Narcissism

The first time that the term "narcissism" was brought to light was in ancient Greek mythology when the tale of Narcissus was passed on to new generations (Braun, 2017). Sigmund Freud also defined narcissism in his work "On Narcissism: Introduction." The author stated that narcissism is an attitude of a person who treats their own body as a sexual object, and he wrote that this trait is significant because it shows perversion (Strachey, 2015). "Narcissism" was defined as a "broad personality construct that included an exaggerated sense of self-importance, fantasies of unlimited success or power, need for admiration, entitlement, lack of empathy, and exploitation of others" (Sharma & Kirkman, 2015, p. 206). Narcissistic personality traits, and more so NPD, have been defined in the DSM-5. NPD is characterized by the following features: "arrogance, power, entitlement, brilliance, beauty, attention-seeking, lack of empathy, grandiosity, and depression," as well as many others (Morey & Stanger, 2012). The proposed research on the perception of a narcissistic leader in the organization has based its finding on the suggested definitions, including negative and positive features of narcissistic individuals.

A Leader in Organizations

The crucial aspect of the presented research was the link between the narcissistic individual and leadership; thus, some of the personality traits characteristic of a narcissist have been desired among good leaders. This study has divided the organization's leaders into those who have the "darker" traits of NPD and those who have the "brighter" traits. According to Nevicka et al. (2018), the personality traits of a good leader (the bright side) are enthusiasm, charisma, attractive vision, sense of humor, and personal charm. Leaders with these traits have been associated with success and power. Nevertheless, some leaders have a dark side, especially when possessing some characteristics of a narcissistic personality. The research has followed the negative models of the narcissistic leader presented by Grijalva et al. (2015). Such a model defined a leader as being an antagonist, egocentric, entitled to everything, lacking empathy, and being "less likely to place the needs of others above their own needs selflessly" (Grijalva et al., 2014).

Methods of Leader Evaluation

The purpose of the given research was to measure a narcissistic leader's perception in the organization following specific forms of leader evaluation. The critical component was the forms of assessments taken under consideration for the study such as the self-evaluations and assessments by others. According to Braun (2017), the self-evaluations are conducted by the narcissistic leader, and the others' evaluations are performed by other employees such as coworkers, subordinates, or followers. It is necessary to distinguish between these two because they are differently correlated with the perception of the narcissistic leader. Grijalva and Newman (2015) stated that in organizations, employee evaluation has usually been executed via a questionnaire or survey, which could be done through email, on paper, or during face-to-face interviews. These were also the criteria that were used when selecting articles for this research.

Organization of Doctoral Project

The topic of the research chapter was the perception of a narcissistic leader in an organization. The subject matter's main focus was to analyze the opinion of a narcissistic leader in the organization, following employee evaluation forms. The research was based on literature reviews of existing articles that discussed narcissism and leadership in organizations.

The chapter contains information on the background, a statement of the problems, and the study's purpose. The literature has shown that numerous studies have been already conducted on this topic. However, none of the articles discussed the forms of employee evaluation and their impact on how the narcissistic leader was perceived by employees. The research was based on an article review of already-existing data on narcissism, narcissistic personality traits, narcissistic leaders, the perception of narcissism, and forms of evaluation of narcissistic leaders in organizations. The research method used was qualitative with a focus on the retrospective causal-comparative method. In this type of comparative analysis, the researcher investigated a research question after the effects already occurred. The researcher studied how one variable may have influenced another variable. In this instance, the research examined how the various forms of evaluation of narcissistic leaders affected a narcissistic leader's perception of the organization and employees' well-being.

This form of research method was the most appropriate for the proposed topic; many articles have already been published examining narcissistic leaders in an organization, which have given a good overview of how the leaders' coworkers and subordinates perceived the leader.

The research was based on these findings and extended the topic to show that the perception of such leaders is linked with the form of evaluation and that this impacts the outcomes of such behavior by negatively affecting other employees, especially the ones from the lower level. The literature review also shows that such leaders' narcissistic behaviors have a very negative effect on employees of a given organization, causing significant levels of stress and lack of job motivation, lowering effectiveness and job satisfaction, and, in some cases, causing people to resign from work.

The following part of the research was the summary of the results and discussion. The study has shown that a narcissistic leader's perception is closely related to the form of employee evaluation used in organizations. The other aspect of the research has shown that when the narcissistic leader had to self-evaluate themselves, their opinion of themselves as leaders has always been higher than that of others and positive. However, if the leaders' subordinates had done the assessment, there was always a negative perception of the narcissistic leader. The last part of the research has examined the impact that the opinion of narcissistic leaders might have on the leader-follower relationship.

References

American Psychiatric Association. (2013). *Diagnostic and Statistical Manual of Mental Disorders (DSM-5®)*, Fifth Edition. https://www.appi.org/Diagnostic_and_Statistical_Manual_of_Mental_Disorders_DSM-5_Fifth_Edition

Baars, S. (2015). Narcissistic leadership. https://docplayer.net/56209673-Narcissistic-leadership.html

Biolcati, R., & Passini, S. (2018). Narcissism and self-esteem: Different motivations for selfie posting behaviors. *Cogent Psychology* 5: 1. https://www.cogentoa.com/article/10.1080/23311908.2018.1437012

Blair, C., Helland, C., & Walton, B. (2017). Leaders behaving badly: The relationship between narcissism and unethical leadership. *Leadership & Organization Development Journal* 38(2): 333–346. http://www.citethisforme.com/topic-ideas/business-marketing/Employee%20Engagement-45397041

Blair, C., Hoffman, B., & Helland, K. (2008). Narcissism in organizations: A multisource appraisal reflects different perspectives. *Human Performance* 21(3): 254–276. https://link.springer.com/chapter/10.1007/978-3-319-60330-8_4

Braun, S. (2017). Leader narcissism and outcomes in organizations: A review at multiple levels of analysis and implications for future research. *Frontiers in Psychology* 8: 773. https://www.frontiersin.org/articles/10.3389/fpsyg.2017.00773/full

Braun, S., Aydin, N., Frey, D., & Peus, C. (2016). Leader narcissism predicts malicious envy and supervisor-targeted counterproductive work behavior – evidence from field and experimental research. *Journal of Business Ethics* 151: 725–741. http://dro.dur.ac.uk/18920/

Cullen, K., Gentry, W., & Yammarino, F. (2015). Biased self-perception tendencies: Self-enhancement/self-diminishment and leader derailment in individualistic and collectivistic cultures. *Applied Psychology* 64: 161–207. http://onlinelibrary.wiley.com/resolve/doi?DOI=10.1111%2Fapps.12026

Foster, D., Campbell, K., & Twenge, J. (2003). Individual differences in narcissism: Inflated self-views across the lifespan and around the world. *Journal of Research in Personality* 37: 469–486. https://www.sciencedirect.com/science/article/pii/S0092656603000266

Galvin, B., Lange, D., & Ashforth, B. (2014). Narcissistic organizational identification: Seeing oneself as central to the organization's identity. *Academy of Management Review* 40. https://journals.aom.org/doi/abs/10.5465/amr.2013.0103

Gnambs, T., & Appel, M. (2017). Narcissism and social networking behavior: A meta-analysis. *Journal of Personality* 86: 200–212. https://onlinelibrary.wiley.com/doi/abs/10.1111/jopy.12305

Grijalva, E., Harms, P., Newman, D., Gaddis, B., & Fraley, R. (2014). Narcissism and leadership: A meta-analytic review of linear and nonlinear relationships. *Personnel Psychology* 68: 1–47. https://onlinelibrary.wiley.com/doi/abs/10.1111/peps.12072

Grijalva, E., & Newman, D. (2015). Narcissism and counterproductive work behavior (CWB): Meta-analysis and consideration of collectivist culture, big five personality, and narcissism's facet structure. *Applied Psychology* 64: 93–126. https://experts.illinois.edu/en/publications/narcissism-and-counterproductive-work-behavior-cwb-meta-analysis-

Hart, W., Adams, J., Burton, A., & Tortoriello, G. (2017). Narcissism and self-presentation: Profiling grandiose and vulnerable narcissists' self-presentation tactic use. *Personality and Individual Differences* 104: 48–57. https://www.sciencedirect.com/science/article/abs/pii/S0191886916308121. https://link.springer.com/article/10.1007/s10551-012-1296-4

Hua-Qiang, Guang-Lei, & Zhi-Hui. (2018). How supervisor narcissism contributes to employee silence: Roles of negative anticipations and leader–member exchange. *Social Behavior and Personality* 46(4): 653–666. https://www.sbp-journal.com/index.php/sbp/article/view/6815

Keller Hansbrough, T., & Jones, G. (2014). Inside the minds of narcissists: How narcissistic leaders' cognitive processes contribute to abusive supervision. *Zeitschrift für Psychologie* 222(4): 214–220. https://econtent.hogrefe.com/doi/10.1027/2151-2604/a000188

Korhonen, J. (2017, January 01). Effects of narcissistic leadership on organizational citizenship behaviors: A case study on the perceptions of media production company employees. http://jultika.oulu.fi/Record/nbnfioulu-201705252103

Mainah, F., & Perkins, V. (2016). Narcissism in organizational leadership. http://www.docdatabase.net/more-narcissism-in-organizational-leadership-fredah-mainah--1327285.html

Meurs, A., Fox, S., Kessler, S., & Spector, P. (2013). It's all about me: The role of narcissism in exacerbating the relationship between stressors and counterproductive work behavior. *Work & Stress* 27(4): 368–382. https://www.tandfonline.com/doi/full/10.1080/02678373.2013.84977

Morey, L., & Stagner, B. (2012). Narcissistic pathology as core personality dysfunction: Comparing the DSM-IV and the DSM-5 proposal for narcissistic personality disorder. *Journal of Clinical Psychology* 68: 908–921. https://onlinelibrary.wiley.com/doi/abs/10.1002/jclp.21895

Nevicka, B., De Hoogh, A. H., Van Vianen, A. E., & Ten Velden, F. S. (2013). Uncertainty enhances the preference for narcissistic leaders. *European Journal of Social Psychology* 43: 370–380. https://www.narcis.nl/publication/RecordID/oai%3Adare.uva.nl%3Apublications%2F84d8e93b-f2a0-41f4-9475-20a793aeb194

Nevicka, B., Hartog, D., & De Hoogh, A. (2016). Gender differences in the perceived effectiveness of narcissistic leaders. *Applied Psychology* 64: 473–498. https://onlinelibrary.wiley.com/doi/abs/10.1111/apps.12015

Nevicka, B., Van Vianen, A., De Hoogh, A., & Voorn, B. (2018). Narcissistic leaders: An asset or a liability? Leader visibility, follower responses, and group-level absenteeism. *Journal of Applied Psychology* 103: 703–723. https://dare.uva.nl/personal/search?identifier=3206d78e-0bdd-43d2-9ba5-98c5d2cd6157

Nevicka, B., Velden, F., Hoogh, A., & Vianen, A. (2011). Reality at odds with perceptions: Narcissistic leaders and group performance. *Psychological Science* 22: 1259–1264. https://journals.sagepub.com/doi/10.1177/0956797611417259

Owens, B., Wallace, A., & Waldman, D. (2015). Leader narcissism and follower outcomes: The counterbalancing effect of leader humility. *Journal of Applied Psychology* 100: 1203–1213. https://asu.pure.elsevier.com/en/publications/leader-narcissism-and-follower-outcomes-the-counterbalancing-effe

Schilling, J., & Schyns, B. (2015). The causes and consequences of bad leadership. *Zeitschrift für Psychologie* 222(4): 187–189. https://doi.org/10.1027/2151-2604/a000185

Sharma, N., & Kirkman, B. (2015). Leveraging leaders: A literature review and future lines of inquiry for empowering leadership research. *Group & Organization Management* 40: 193–237. https://journals.sagepub.com/doi/full/10.1177/1059601115574906

Strachey, J. (ed) (2015). *The Standard Edition of the Complete Psychological Works of Sigmund Freud* (Vol. 1–24). https://www.amazon.com/Complete-Psychological-Works-Sigmund-Standard/dp/0393011283

2 Narcissisms in Leadership – Its Essence and Classification

A Literature Review

Narcissism is a set of personality traits that characterize a very dynamic, visionary, decisive person with a strong desire for admiration (Nevicka et al., 2013). Such a person is self-centered, dominant, despotic, extroverted, and lacking in empathy (Keller Hansbrough & Jones, 2014; Owens, Wallace, & Waldman, 2015; Zhi-Hui et al., 2018). Researchers have noticed that the number of narcissists has been rising in the population. Among the general population, around 6.2% of people have narcissistic traits, including 7.7% of men and 4.8% of women (George & Short, 2018). People diagnosed with this personality disorder or expressing narcissistic traits have often been chosen by organizations to become leaders (Baars, 2015; Braun, 2017; Grijalva et al., 2015; Nevicka et al., 2018a). Researchers have distinguished between grandiose narcissism, which is associated with one having a favorable opinion of oneself, and vulnerable narcissism, which is linked with the fear of being criticized or spoken badly about (Grijalva et al., 2015; Hart et al., 2017: Nevicka et al., 2018a). The type of narcissism and the more distinguished traits in a given individual determine whether the narcissistic leader is perceived as a dark or bright person.

Previous research has also found that many narcissistic leaders in organizations have been perceived in a negative light, especially by their employees (Galvin, Lange, & Ashforth, 2014; Korhonen, 2017; Mainah & Perkins, 2016). This also reflects on leader-employee relations in a given company. However, there were also signs that a significantly lower number of workers have positive opinions about narcissism. The different and very diverse opinions on narcissistic leaders could be linked with the type of narcissistic leader evaluation and, more closely, with the group of responders of the evaluation form. This study aimed to test the perception of a narcissistic leader in organizations with correlation to various employee assessment types. Research from the literature review has examined how different types of leader evaluations affect a narcissistic leader's opinion in an organization. The study's aim was to show the forms of narcissistic leader evaluations used in organizations. Special attention has been placed on self-assessments and other-reports. The next step of the research was to investigate the impact that a given evaluation method had on the

DOI: 10.4324/9781003260646-2

narcissistic leader's perception. Lastly, the study analyzed the influence that a negatively perceived narcissistic leader has on their employees and subordinates.

Literature Search Strategy

The research has linked narcissistic personality traits with the leadership role and presents the positive and negative opinion of such a leader. This study has presented information on how the narcissistic leader was perceived in an organization and whether this perception was positive or negative. How does the perception of a narcissistic leader in an organization change when analyzing the various forms of leader evaluation? The research was based on the literature review of existing articles on narcissistic leaders' topic in organizations. The publications chosen for this research were only retrieved from the online databases by searching through the school libraries and other online journals. The main criterion for inclusion was that the articles had to be scholarly and peer-reviewed ones from academic journals to ensure the quality of research. The time frame set for the publications ranged from 1914 to 2019. The reports were extracted from the University of Southern California database, and the leading search engine used for the research was EBSCO Host. The articles' search was divided into three categories. The first search aimed to select articles concerning information on the narcissistic leader evaluation methods used in organizations. The second search criterion of inclusion for publications targeted the second problem studied in the research: the perception of a narcissistic leader in an organization. The third search was for articles concerning the outcome or impact that the opinion of narcissistic leaders had on their relationship with their employees.

To examine the first research questions, the articles had to contain information concerning at least one method of evaluation of narcissistic leaders in an organization, such as self-reporting and other reports (Galvin, Lange, & Ashforth, 2014; Grijalva et al., 2015; Hart et al., 2017; Nevicka et al., 2018b; Schyns & Schilling, 2012). The criteria for inclusion consisted of a combination of words, as follows: "methods of employee evaluation in organizations," "narcissistic leader evaluation methods," "forms of narcissistic leader assessment," "levels of analysis," as well as other combinations of these words. This search revealed that the form of leaders in organizations had usually been assessed through self-reports and other reports mainly conducted by subordinates, followers, or significant others of narcissistic leaders. The literature indicated that the method of evaluation might have influenced the perception of narcissistic leaders among their employees and followers.

Furthermore, the search revealed that, since narcissistic leaders have various personality traits, they can either be perceived in a positive or negative light (Baars, 2015; Braun, 2017; Grijalva et al., 2015; Nevicka et al.,

2018b). The articles chosen to examine this problem contained information related to the keywords "perception of leaders in an organization," "corporate narcissism," "opinion of the narcissistic leader," as well as other variations of similar words. Recent studies have linked the diverse perception of narcissistic leaders with grandiose narcissism, which leads others to have a negative opinion about the narcissistic leader and the leader to have a positive opinion about themselves (Galvin, Lange, & Ashforth, 2014; Korhonen, 2017; Mainah & Perkins, 2016). In contrast, vulnerable narcissism traits were associated with the narcissist's fear of criticism and their fear of negative opinions about them (Grijalva et al., 2015; Hart et al., 2017; Nevicka et al., 2018a). The form of leaders' assessment in organizations have been performed through self-reports and the other reports mainly conducted by subordinates, followers, or significant others of narcissistic leaders. This information indicates that the method of evaluation might have influenced the perception of narcissistic leaders among their employees and followers.

Researchers have widely studied the topic of narcissistic leaders in the organization in recent times. This topic has mainly been analyzed from the organizational viewpoint, which has demonstrated that narcissists are desired as leaders in organizations because they are assertive and company-oriented (Galvin, Lange, & Ashforth, 2014; Grijalva et al., 2015; Hart et al., 2017; Nevicka et al., 2018b; Mainah & Perkins, 2016; Schyns & Schilling, 2012). Researchers have tested the influence of narcissistic personality traits on the leaders' behavior and actions in organizations, thus also showing the negative side of such individuals. These findings lead one to question the impact that narcissistic leaders have on other employees or their immediate subordinates. The article review showed that although the narcissistic leader's work positively affects the organization in the short run, it negatively affects the leader's relationship with employees and employee outcomes (Nevicka et al., 2011; Ong et al., 2016; Owens, Wallace, & Waldman, 2015). Therefore, the research has examined the correlation between narcissistic leader evaluation and perception of such a leader by their subordinates and other employees. To identify this research, the following keywords were used: "narcissistic leaders and organizational outcome," "influence of narcissistic CEO on employees," "workers outcome," and other variations of those phrases. Although they are considered valuable assets for their company, current research has shown that narcissistic leaders have often harmed other employees, especially their subordinates and followers.

Theoretical Framework

Narcissism has been of interest to various researchers in the past few decades. One of the reasons for this has been an increase in narcissistic personality traits in society. However, narcissism is not solely a modern phenomenon; many famous personas from the past also possessed narcissistic personality traits. Some had incredible charisma and led people or countries to glories, such as Napoleon Bonaparte, Franklin Delano Roosevelt, or Mahatma Gandhi (Maccoby, 2014). Simultaneously, destructive and selfish ones caused wars and mass devastation among humanity, such as Hitler, Stalin, or Saddam Hussein (Rosenthal, 2010). The previous studies have shown that narcissists can possess both positive and negative personality traits associated with narcissism and use them to either do good or ruin everyone due to their distorted vision of the world. Hence, there is a need to group all the narcissistic personality features to create the theory of the narcissistic individual and narcissistic leaders in an organization. To understand this issue, it is essential to understand the origin, development, and theory of narcissism. The next aspect was to present narcissism in leadership and how the subordinates and the leaders perceive the narcissistic leader.

Historical Background

To analyze narcissism, one must understand its roots. These show that people have expressed narcissistic personality traits long before specialists labeled them as such and related them to specific individuals. Narcissism comes from Greek mythology, where the nymph Echo punished a handsome young boy for rejecting her by making him fascinated with his beauty and reflection. Falling in love with his beauty, the boy rejected the attention of everyone surrounding him and rejected self-love (Braun, 2017; Fatfouta, 2019; Rosenthal, 2010). The myth presents some of a narcissistic person's core characteristics: affection for self-love, preoccupation with oneself, and antagonistic relationship with other people. Until the 19th century, any reference to narcissism was connected to the mentioned mythological story. The first person to find psychological inspiration in the Greek myth was Havelock Ellis (Grenyer, 2013). In his paper, Ellis described the case of a woman who became lost in self-admiration, symbolized by the mirror. As Grenyer (2013) described, Ellis conceived narcissism as autoeroticism or the self-absorption of sexual emotion into self-admiration. Ellis's contributions furthered the pathological aspects of people's understanding of narcissism. Ellis's discussion also covered group psychology by explaining how people endorse national narcissism, patriotism, and the hatred of foreigners. Later, Paul Näcke, a Russian-born German psychiatrist and director of an asylum in Colditz, Saxony, was the first to introduce the term "narcissism" to psychiatry in 1899 in a study of sexual perversions, particularly excessive masturbation (Grenyer, 2013).

The next person to mention narcissism in his work was Sigmund Freud, who spoke of narcissism in his early work "Three Essays on the Theory of Sexuality" (Rosenthal, 2010). Later, Freud dedicated an entire treatise to narcissism as psychological dysfunction titled "On Narcissism: An Introduction" (Strachey, 2015). Freud conceptualized narcissism as pathological self-love for one's body. His ideas were the precursor of narcissism's psychodynamic theory, which emphasizes the early interactions between infants and their caretakers as the core cause of narcissism (Strachey, 2015). Freud also discovered that a specific set of personality traits, such as confidence, arrogance, and unflappable strength, were simultaneously expressed by this particular type of person.

At the time when Freud defined narcissism as a set of negative traits and behaviors, Ernest Jones pointed out that individuals who had a "God-complex" also displayed positive characteristics such as being "aloof, inaccessible, self-admiring, self-important, overconfident, auto-erotic, and exhibitionistic, with fantasies of omnipotence and omniscience" (Simpson, 2012, p. 2). William Reich added to the theory of narcissism by arguing that a person with narcissistic personality traits was arrogant, mildly sadistic in their relationship, confident, and felt superior to others (Simpson, 2012). Reich was the first psychoanalyst who discussed how narcissists became aggressive when they felt their ego was threatened and who wrote that this disorder was more prominent in men than women. Otto Kornberg and Heinz Kohut followed Freud's footsteps and further developed narcissism theory to describe it as a personality disorder or pathology (Rosenthal, 2010). Kornberg evaluated narcissists as patients who differ from others because they present a lack of empathy and are charmful and exploitative, lead shallow emotional lives, devaluate others, envy others, and have an inflated self-concept (Rosenthal, 2010). He assumed that these traits could be explained through pathological regression from their distant parents or an aggressive rejection of them. However, Kohut emphasized that narcissism first develops in childhood and can either be healthy or mature narcissism, which is related to higher creativity, or pathological narcissism, which is linked with one's unhealthy idealization (Simpson, 2012).

The research on narcissism started to advance in the 1980s when scholars examined the subject from a clinical perspective and termed it a personality disorder. The clinical theory of narcissism has been described by the American Psychological Association (APA). The term narcissism was defined for the first time in the Diagnostic and Statistical Manual of Mental Disorders IV (DSM-IV) as a psychological disorder (Foster, Campbell, & Twenge, 2003; Stinson et al., 2008). The DSM-5 currently defines the main personality traits in narcissistic personality disorder (NPD) as including "arrogance, power, entitlement, brilliance, beauty, attention-seeking, lack of empathy, grandiosity, and depression" (Morey & Stagner, 2012). People suspected to have NPD have been submitted to tests and are diagnosed with it if they score five out of nine in the DSM-5 criteria, or without NPD if they did not meet the requirements.

Narcissism

When analyzing narcissism, the most important factor to consider is understand the many faces of narcissism, which are associated with the personality characteristics of a given individual and a personality disorder. Narcissism could be perceived as a personality disorder, NPD (Foster, Campbell, & Twenge, 2003), or a set of narcissistic personality traits (Nevicka et al., 2018b). NPD is a clinical theory that argues that people who meet the list of behaviors associated with NPD included in the DSM-5 criteria are narcissists (Morey & Stagner, 2012). These criteria include having a grandiose sense of self-importance, lacking empathy, needing excessive admiration, having a sense of entitlement, demonstrating interpersonally exploitative behavior, being envious of others, being arrogant, brilliant, and charming, and believing in one's power and success (Braun, 2017). The personality variables of narcissism include narcissism, Machiavellianism, and psychopathy, and each variable can vary from low to high (Fatfouta, 2019). Individuals with narcissistic personality traits as described in the social conception of narcissism have negative personalities. Thus, most of the time, they exhibit negative behaviors that are harmful to people around them. Some of these features are angry outbursts, public ridiculing, abusive behavior, and hostile supervision (Keller Hansbrough & Jones, 2014). Such individuals are also oversensitive to criticism, disregard other people's opinions, and often take credit for others' work (Nevicka et al., 2013). Owens, Wallace, and Waldman (2015) also stated that narcissists have a grandiose sense of self and are self-absorbing. In this study, the researcher used the theory of narcissistic personality traits. Thus, not all narcissistic leaders have been diagnosed or express the strict features of NPD.

Narcissism can be mild or severe, depending on the person's awareness of it and their ability to control it. In this research, two forms of narcissism are recognized: grandiose and vulnerable. These forms exist in the clinical (NPD) and the social theory of narcissistic personality (Furtner et al., 2017). The distinction between grandiose narcissism and vulnerable narcissism was made by Paul Wink (Zajenkowski et al., 2018). The grandiose form is characterized by high self-esteem and a tendency to dominate and exaggerate one's capabilities (Nevicka et al., 2013). Narcissistic individuals on the grandiose spectrum fantasize about their superiority, power, and perfection (Zajenkowski et al., 2018). Grandiose narcissists often exhibit the negative traits of narcissistic personalities such as exploitativeness, ruthlessness, despotism, or manipulativeness (Zhi-Hui et al., 2018). Vulnerable narcissism is associated with being entitled, being self-absorbed, and needing attention. However, as opposed to grandiose narcissism, a person with vulnerable narcissism is shy, passive-aggressive, and has low self-esteem, depression, anxiety, and hypersensitivity, which might be related to their being neglected belittled in the past (Rogoza et al., 2018).

Individuals with vulnerable narcissism features are less likely to negatively influence the people they work with or surround themselves with.

Narcissism and Leadership

Narcissism also gained interest in the aspect of leadership, especially when examining organizations. Researchers have pointed out that some of a narcissist's core features are traits that are desirable in leaders or CEOs of large organizations. This has been called the bright side of being a narcissistic leader (Nevicka et al., 2018b). According to Nevicka et al. (2018a), leaders should have charm, charisma, great vision, and a sense of humor. In Keller Hansbrough and Jones' (2014) theory of a good leader, such a person should help employees during times of uncertainty by being enthusiastic and decisive. Owens, Wallace, and Waldman (2015) have supported the thesis that a good leader should be a risk-taker and persistent in their actions, especially when it comes to achieving personal and company goals. The above characteristics are also typical of narcissists, hence linking narcissistic personality traits and leadership traits. Despite the favorable traits of narcissistic leaders (the positive side), some characteristics leaders have are part of the negative side. Such a person can appear despotic and toxic to the work environment (Zhi-Hui et al., 2018). Some other undesirable traits that are associated with narcissistic traits are arrogance, dominance, oversensitiveness to criticism (Grijalva et al., 2015), greediness for power, and ruthlessness (Nevicka et al., 2013). Such leaders also seek admiration and are manipulative and unethical (Zhi-Hui et al., 2018). Keller Hansbrough and Jones (2014) also noticed that narcissistic leaders take credit for others' work, publicly ridicule their coworkers and followers, and have angry outbursts. For this study's purpose, I examined the mentioned negative side of the narcissistic personality, namely the traits that have been criticized in the literature and that usually harm other employees, subordinates, or colleagues of narcissistic leaders. Examining this side was necessary to establish the ground for the research on employees' perceptions of a narcissistic leader in organizations. The study was based on those characteristics so that narcissistic leaders' particular behaviors were apparent to the audience.

Methods of Leader Evaluation and Perception

The research also analyzed the methods to evaluate narcissistic leaders to measure the correlation between leadership evaluation forms and the perception of a narcissistic leader in an organization. Grijalva et al. (2015) presented various methods of leader assessment in organizations, such as anonymous surveys or questionnaires via email, face-to-face interviews, or written evaluations. However, Braun's (2017) evaluation method of self-reporting and other reporting was used in the following study. The type of reporting is a variable that influences the perception of a narcissistic leader in the organization. The perception of a narcissistic leader in an organization has gone in two directions. Leaders in organizations are either perceived positively or negatively. The positive opinion has been related to the "bright side," that is, the positive personality traits of a narcissist, whereas the negative view has been linked with the dark features (Keller Hansbrough & Jones 2014; Nevicka et al., 2013; Owens, Wallace, & Waldman, 2015). It has also been pointed out that when a narcissistic leader self-evaluates themselves, they put high scores because they speak highly of themselves, often using superlatives (Braun, 2017). However, when other employees assess a narcissistic leader, they are more critical and objective, which leads to an honest but often negative opinion of the leaders (Nevicka et al., 2013; Owens, Wallace, & Waldman, 2015).

Narcissistic Personality Traits

The research's primary purpose was to argue that the way that narcissistic leaders are assessed plays a crucial role in how the leader is perceived in the organization. It has been shown by researchers that narcissistic personality traits are desirable among future leaders. Thus, such people have the strength and charisma to reach career highs and lead the company to the same highs on the market. Research has discussed the source of narcissism and its definition to present an overview of the main features of a narcissist personality. Narcissistic personalities have been linked with a leadership role and the forms of evaluation of such leaders. The study's purpose was to show that the type of leaders' assessment impacts a narcissistic leader's perception in the organization, impacting both the positive and negative impressions. How does the opinion of a narcissistic leader in an organization influence the wellbeing of employees? This study was based on an article review of already-existing data on narcissism, narcissistic personality traits, narcissistic leaders, the perception of narcissism, and forms of evaluation of narcissistic leaders in the organization. The study aimed to show that after performing employee evaluations of narcissistic leaders in organizations make it clear that such leaders are perceived negatively by their subordinates, and the stress related to this perception severely impacts the employees' wellbeing and work effectiveness.

Narcissism has many aspects, which means that it should not be categorized only as NPD but rather divided into subcategories or dimensions depending on the extent to which individuals express certain narcissistic features. In the past, narcissism was studied solely using psychoanalytical and psychodynamic approaches to it (Carter & Douglass, 2018). Narcissism was defined as a disorder for the first time in the third edition of the Diagnostic and Statistical Manual. Still, it was not until the DSM-IV was published that narcissism was classified as a Cluster-B Personality Disorder (Carter & Douglass, 2018). Later, the researchers started to divide narcissism into its clinical and social forms to show that not all individuals who possess narcissistic personality traits should be diagnosed with NPD (Nevicka et al., 2018b). Campbell et al. (2011) named social narcissism the trait narcissism to express its indifference from the NPD. Other researchers have classified narcissism as falling into pathological and normal narcissism (Kiliç & Eryilmaz, 2019; Muller, 2014), whereas others have categorized it as falling into the grandiose and vulnerable dimensions (Ackerman et al., 2011; Jauk et al., 2017; Zajenkowski et al., 2018). Many researchers have claimed that it is best to analyze narcissists in organizational settings by using the social aspect of narcissism, that is, the healthy or normal form of narcissism rather than the pathological or clinical type, NPD (Nevicka et al., 2018b; Campbell et al., 2011).

Defining Narcissism

Grandiose vs. Vulnerable

Narcissism has been categorized as falling into the grandiose and vulnerable categories. Grandiose narcissism has also been named by some specialists as overt (Jauk et al., 2017) or phallic narcissism (Campbell et al., 2011). The etiology of narcissism is multifaceted, which means that there are some genetic predispositions, developmental problems, traumatic childhood events, being rejected as a child or fragile ego in early years. According to Campbell et al. (2011), grandiose narcissism's etiology is being overvalued as a child. Kohut's (1971) states that clinically oriented researchers have proposed that pathological narcissism results from developmental interruption, which results in a psychological (narcissistic) injury that stimulates defense.

Evidence from the recent study shows that remembered childhood experiences of being overprotected, overvalued, and experiencing leniency in parental discipline are associated with higher traits of pathological narcissism in younger generations. In their research, Van Schie et al. (2020) present that parental overprotection is linked to elevated narcissism. The study indicates that overprotection of childless autonomous limits an individual's ability to learn from one's own experiences and makes them more reliant on others for guidance and feedback. It means that a young person may foster entitlement and negative self-beliefs. In addition, such an individual is more prone to develop elevated narcissistic traits. While measuring the correlation between narcissism and overvaluation, Van Schie et al. (2020) discovered that the combination of paternal overvaluation with lack of care for the child's needs plays a key role in the development of elevated narcissism in young adults. The researchers have also studied the correlation between maternal and paternal care in developing narcissism in young adults. The research shows that remembered maternal care or childhood maltreatment is related to traits of vulnerable but not grandiose narcissism (Van Schie et al., 2020). However, the measurements of paternal care in the development of narcissism present a protective factor in both forms of narcissism.

Betrayal is also accounted as one of the cause of narcissism. Yalch and Levendosky (2019) express in their study that exposure to high betrayal trauma inflicts a psychological wound (narcissistic vulnerability). Researchers also add that betrayal by a close person such as a parent, guardian, or someone a child trusts influences how people defend against that wound (narcissistic grandiosity). Exposure to a betrayal trauma was also found to cause other personality disorders such as psychopathy, which is also linked with narcissism. Yalch and Levendosky (2019) explain that both narcissists and psychopaths express similar coping mechanisms in the form of aggression to regulate their weakness and internal feelings. Washburn and Paskar (2011) present that culture also has a significant impact on narcissism in individuals. Authors have examined that people from more individualistic cultures express more narcissistic behavior in oppose to people from collective orientation (Washburn & Paskar, 2011).

Genetics also plays an important role in etiology of narcissism. Luo and Cai (2018) present in their study that in the United States and Canada variations in narcissism were mainly explained by genetic factors (59%) and in China (47%) were hereditary. Findings from the literature review suggest that about half of the variation of grandiose narcissism can be attributed to genetic influence.

Grandiose Narcissism

Grandiose narcissism is also labeled the oblivious narcissism due to individual's lack of insight on impact that they have on others. Researchers have noted that the most individuals with common traits of this form of narcissism are having an arrogant attitude and an inflated sense of self-esteem and being exploitative, entitled, and exhibitionist (Ackerman et al., 2011; Miller et al., 2012; Zajenkowski et al., 2018). People with grandiose narcissism are also socially bold extroverts who can be charming when the situation requires it (Jauk et al., 2017). Individuals diagnosed with grandiose narcissism have been linked to psychopathy and antisocial personality (Campbell et al., 2011).

In interpersonal relations, grandiose narcissists are dominant, manipulative (Campbell et al., 2011; Miller et al., 2012), and aggressive toward their subordinates or friends and family, and refuse to comply with authority (Miller et al., 2012). Carter and Douglas (2018) have also noted that such individuals have maladaptive traits that result in an inability to maintain romantic and social relationships. Their constant need for attention and glory often pushes partners away (Campbell et al., 2011). As Bilotta et al. (2018) state, people with grandiose narcissism lack empathy and subjective distress, which are related to their impaired understanding of their mental states and the mental states of others. When threatened by a partner to break up, the grandiose narcissist may be able to modulate their vulnerability by promoting themselves (e.g., reporting positive things about themselves). However, it is only a short-term coping mechanism, used by narcissists to prevent the breakup. A study has shown that in the long term, the fantasy of superiority (Zajenkowski et al., 2018) and the disagreeableness demonstrated by grandiose narcissists become more vivid, which leads to a loss of popularity and lack of interaction with their acquaintances (Czarna, Dufner, & Clifton, 2014).

When it comes to the social contacts, grandiose narcissists initiate many superficial social contacts. They excel in self-promotion as long as the social contact remains superficial (Brailovskaia et al., 2020). Such people also often receive positive feedback from the people they interact with as long as the interaction partners are unable to sense the selfishness as narcissistic person, lack of empathy, and manipulation. The positive feedback reassures narcissists in their grandiosity, perfection, and superiority over others (Zajenkowski et al., 2018). Their self-esteem is high and is linked to subjective optimism, life satisfaction, and happiness (Brailovskaia et al., 2020). In the organizational setting, grandiose narcissists have significant impact on workers' well-being, especially if they hold leadership positions. Wirtz and Rigotti (2020) mentioned in their empirical study that grandiose narcissism was strongly positively related to competitiveness.

The most typical characteristic of grandiose narcissism is that its traits are oriented around the overinflated self-worth. Researchers have placed having an inflated self-esteem or high self-esteem in this group of features (Ackerman et al., 2011; Zajenkowski et al., 2018), as well as overconfidence (Campbell et al., 2011), having a strong self-focus, and having an unrealistically positive self-view (Czarna, Dufner, & Clifton, 2014). Studies have also reported that grandiose narcissists express some other specific maladaptive features such as dishonesty, greed, and insincerity (Giacomin, 2016). Such individuals do not take criticism well and are very arrogant when someone tries to tell them they are wrong (Ackerman et al., 2011; Miller et al., 2012). These features indicate that grandiose-narcissistic individuals can be self-centered, apodictic, snooty, and very unpleasant to be around.

Besser and Priel (2010) have defined grandiose narcissism as defensive and unhealthy. Authors have indicated that people with grandiose narcissism are highly engaged in promoting their hypervigilant and self-perceived superiority so that they can detect and eliminate any potential danger to their grandiose self-perceptions (Besser and Priel, 2010). For example, grandiose-narcissistic individuals engage in direct competition with others and often use self-protective behaviors, such as devaluation and derogation, when facing a better performing person. In addition, when the grandiose narcissists don't win, they use externalizing behavior to blame others for their failure or shortcomings. It is also related to their inability to control their emotions (Wolven, 2015). It is because grandiose narcissists value the competition to enhance their self-esteem, hence the anger when they fail to win as number one.

However, grandiose narcissists are charismatic and possess a good sense of leadership, making them excellent leaders (Giacomin, 2016). Furthermore, they are outgoing, making them socially attractive (Carter & Douglas, 2018). They also have excellent interpersonal skills; therefore, they make a great first impression and may seem like good friends to have (Campbell et al., 2011). Grandiose narcissists have the ability to express positive psychological outcomes. Maciantowicz and Zajenkowski (2020) presented in their study that grandiose narcissists can demonstrate positive behavior such as high levels of well-being and low levels of depression loneliness, sadness, and feeling anxious. Due to those features, many grandiose narcissists don't appear to be related to negative effects of aggression or anger. The immense acts of aggression result from situational action, which causes a threat to their narcissistic ego. Those are the defense mechanisms when someone questions their decision, rather than anger toward the world or humanity in general (Maciantowicz & Zajenkowski, 2020).

Grandiose narcissists are also considered a good asset in organizational settings. The studies regarding narcissistic leadership in the organization have shown that grandiose narcissists have positive relationships with crisis management, public persuasiveness, agenda-setting (Nevicka et al., 2015). Furthermore, researchers have noticed that such individuals are excellent in impression management (Wirtz & Rigotti, 2020), leadership emergence (Brunell et al., 2008; Nevicka et al., 2011), and compensation (O'Reilly et al., 2014). Chatterjee and Hambrick (2007) suggest that grandiose narcissistic leaders tend to set ambitious goals and make bold decisions, considered a desirable quality in a leader.

Vulnerable Narcissism

Some of the characteristics are similar for both grandiose and vulnerable narcissism. Zajenkowski et al. (2018) noticed that those two forms of narcissism share the same features such as exaggerated sense of self-importance, disagreeableness, entitlement, self-centeredness, and interaction with other people in antagonistic fashion. This means that they interact with people in a cold and hostile manner.

Vulnerable narcissism is also called "closet narcissism," hypervigilant narcissism, hypersensitive, and covert narcissism (Fennimore, 2020). Some specialists consider vulnerable narcissism as being clinical and antisocial version of this personality abnormality when compared to grandiose narcissism (Rogoza et al., 2018). As noticed by Day and his colleagues (2020), in terms of nomological network, the vulnerable dimension of narcissism has been linked with personal pathology similar to borderline personality disorder (BPD). Scientists also noticed that vulnerable narcissism is related to some features characteristic of internalizing disorders, including depression, anxiety, distrust, paranoia, schizotypy, hostility, low self-esteem, and extreme sensitivity to criticism and rejection, with a similar nomological network to neuroticism (Miller et al., 2012; Wink and Gough, 1990; Kaufman et al., 2020). Although some characteristics of the two types of narcissism are shared, vulnerable narcissism traits vary slightly from grandiose narcissism traits. The etiology of vulnerable narcissism has a different background than that of grandiose narcissism. Campbell et al. (2011) stated that vulnerable narcissism came from parental coldness.

Researchers have noticed that on the matter of self-esteem, vulnerable narcissists have fragile self-esteem (Ackerman et al., 2011) or low self-esteem (Campbell et al., 2011, Czarna, Dufner, & Clifton, 2014), and they often are highly reactive when evaluating events (Czarna, Dufner, & Clifton, 2014). These individuals also actively protect their fragile egos because they are hypersensitive (Zajenkowski et al., 2018). Vulnerable narcissism is also correlated with various types of anger, such as internalization, externalization, and poor anger control, opposed to grandiose narcissism. Such individuals are also more responsive to provocation with high chronic anger and attack toward their responder. Maciantowicz and Zajenkowski (2020) suggest that chronic anger is fueled mainly by distrust and shame; when combined is a dangerous weapon.

Furthermore, evidence shows that vulnerable narcissism is lined with psychopathy and associated with neurotic and antagonistic components of narcissism. The research suggests that antagonism is a primary cause of self-hate guilt, abnormal views of self, world, and future, maladaptive action patterns, and anxious and avoidant attachment style (Kaufman et al., 2020). In addition, Kaufman and colleagues (2020, p 124) found in their study that "self-uncertainty and inauthenticity among those scoring higher in vulnerable narcissism, including higher levels of impostor syndrome, weak sense of self, self-alienation, accepting external influence, and low self-esteem." Researchers also mention that the above determinants hinder the quality of life of narcissistic individual, such as autonomy, life satisfaction, personal growth, authentic living, purpose, self-acceptance, positive relations, and environmental mastery (Miller et al., 2012).

Research has provided evidence that vulnerable narcissists have a problematic attachment style when interacting with society, their close friends, and family (Miller et al., 2012). Furthermore, vulnerable narcissists become defensive (Jauk et al., 2017) and hostile (Miller et al., 2012) when someone wrongly evaluates them because they are vigilant of any criticism (Zajenkowski et al., 2018). Covert narcissisms become vindictive and impose retaliation to those who try to criticize their work or leadership (Fennimore, 2020). However, at the same time, they looked for admiration and recognition. It has also been reported that such individuals are socially avoidant (Czarna, Dufner, & Clifton, 2014), passive-aggressive to others, and show great mistrust toward the people surrounding them (Rogaza et al., 2018). These findings indicate that it might be difficult for vulnerable narcissists to have close relationships with others.

Various studies demonstrate that vulnerable narcissists express territorial behaviors such as ownership of an object in social and organizational settings. Such individuals also have significant tendencies to misperceive neutral social cues as territorial threats or infringements. Fennimore (2020, p. 4) claims that "the vulnerable narcissistic personality features such as hyper-focus, defensiveness and displaying the victim role suggest that these individuals would mark and defend boundaries in organizational territories more aggressively than others." Those findings indicate that covert narcissists get angry quickly when a coworker of a cleaning crew accidentally moves some objects from their desk or when a coworker gets credit for work. Vulnerable narcissists treat it as a personal attack in their territory and may want to regain their territory or power with it. The researcher states that closet narcissists look at those cases as office injustice and respond by retaliating and gossiping about a supervisor, using discriminatory language toward a coworker, or even engaging in illegal activities such as fraud or theft of organizational property (Fennimore, 2020). Narcissists consider objects as the "self," thinking that what is mine becomes a part of me. Resolving conflicts with a vulnerable narcissist over territorial possession is difficult; thus, such individuals act as their integrity is threatened.

The literature has shown that vulnerable narcissists have a great variety of traits that suggest proneness to depressive states. Such people are characterized by increased negative emotionality (Zajenkowski et al., 2018) and linked with pessimistic views of the past and fatalistic attitudes (Miller et al., 2012). They also believe that the entire world is against them (Campbell et al., 2011); therefore, they feel depleted most of the time (Czarna et al. a., 2014). In addition, vulnerably narcissistic individuals hold a negative view of the future, with significantly lower optimism as well as reduced expectations of recovery and career satisfaction (Kaufman et al., 2020). Such individuals also seemed less invested in their personal growth to improve their future perspectives. Researchers found this behavior related to vulnerable narcissists' reluctance to any form of therapy (Kaufman et al., 2020). Furthermore, as reported by Miller et al. (2012), vulnerable narcissists experience anxiety and depression associated with high neuroticism. Previous research has also demonstrated that vulnerable narcissists express deep feelings of inferiority, incompetence, and inadequacy (Czarna, Dufner, & Clifton, 2014). All those features indicate that such individuals are emotionally unstable and might be psychologically dysfunctional, which might have eventually lead to poor well-being (Rogoza et al., 2018). Some authors also believe that this form of narcissism is linked to BPD (Campbell et al., 2011).

The robust empirical study shows that vulnerable narcissism is associated with a negative view of the future. It is a crucial element when diagnosing a narcissistic individual; thus, it also allows assessing such a person's readiness for therapy. Kaufman et al. (2020) mentioned that people who have a negative view of the future are generally pessimistic and have low career satisfaction and life expectations. Furthermore, vulnerable narcissists express a low need for self-growth, which may be an obstacle in getting treatment. Those findings indicate that such people are not interested in improving their future selves; therefore, they may not see a need to attend therapy to enhance their well-being (Kaufman et al., 2020).

Researchers have noticed that grandiose and vulnerable narcissism have some traits in common. Some of the most visible characteristics are an exaggerated sense of self-importance, entitlement, disagreeableness, and interacting with others in antagonistic manners (Zajenkowski et al., 2018). It was examined by Krizan and Herlache (2017) that both variations of narcissism are associated with a lack of empathy toward others, a low need for intimacy, and impaired thinking. Both forms share a sense of entitlement, exploitative behavior, antagonism, and low levels of agreeableness (Miller et al., 2012; Wink and Gough, 1990). Nevertheless, it is necessary to distinguish between these two main types of narcissism when examining narcissistic leaders' aspects.

New studies have shown that there is a relationship between vulnerable narcissism and activity on social media platforms. The results of these studies indicated that persons with enhanced levels of vulnerable narcissism intensively interact with others on Facebook (Brailovskaia et al., 2020). Such a person frequently writes private messages, uploads photos and settings, updates status, and comments on other things. Researchers have stated that the lack of face-to-face contact on social media and the ability to plan and control one's self-presentation more comprehensively than one could in offline interactions might reduce the defensiveness and shyness of vulnerable narcissists in social relations. Brailovskaia et al. (2020) have stated that the levels of anxiety present among vulnerable narcissists decreased significantly on social media due to the relatively high levels of control and predictability of their actions.

Pathological vs. Normal

Kiliç and Eryilmaz (2019) spoke of narcissism as having two dimensions: the pathological and normal dimensions. Wirtz and Rigotti (2020) name those two dimensions as the clinical and subclinical. The difference between subclinical and clinical levels of narcissism lies mainly in the consequences for the affected individual. Clinical narcissism causes "functional impairment or subjective distress" (American Psychiatric Association, 2013), which does not apply for subclinical narcissism. Pathological narcissism is considered a personality disorder as NPD. Kiliç and Eryilmaz (2019) claim that individuals with pathological narcissism are characterized by extreme confidence, anger, aggression, antisocial behavior, a non-caring attitude toward others, or showed inconvenience when their value is not appreciated or noticed by others (Kiliç & Eryilmaz, 2019). Muller (2014) spoke of pathological narcissism as the most severe form of narcissism; thus, people with this pathology are oversensitive to criticism, overcontrolling, over-competitive, and lie and exaggerate frequently. Ackerman et al. (2011) named pathological narcissism as a set of maladaptive self-regulatory processes that lead to impairment and significant distress of a given individual.

Muller (2014) also added a third category of malignant narcissism (MN). It is the grandiose dimension of narcissism that is often associated with pathological form of it. Erich Fromm first used the term "malignant narcissist" in 1964 as a severe mental disorder (Goldner-Vukov & Moore, 2010). Later, the term MN was introduced to psychiatric literature by Otto Kernberg in the early 1980s (Lane & Kent, 2008). A definition of the malignant narcissist ascribes such individuals as people who "experience increased self-esteem and confirmation of their grandiosity when they can express aggression toward themselves and others" (Lane & Kent, 2008). Kernberg also distinguished four basic characteristics of MN: ego-syntonic sadism, antisocial behavior, a typical core NPD, and a deeply paranoid orientation to life (Goldner-Vukov & Moore, 2010). The ego-syntonic sadism consisted of aggressive self-affirmation, which was present in destruction, castration, and dehumanization of other people. MN is fueled with the desire for revenge and sometimes proceeds with suicide when during a crisis. To them, it is a form of triumph, and they become the masters of their fate. Kernberg also stated that people with MN have paranoid tendencies which are expressed in the form of distrust and viewing others as enemies or idiots, while devaluating them. They are also engaged in the conspiracy theories, which may lead to incidents of psychosis. Goldner-Vukov and Moore (2010) also mentioned that individuals with MN tend to lie, steal, and commit burglary assault or even murder somebody. Very often such individuals become leaders of terroristic or sadistic groups.

The other main features that predispose individuals to this pathology are reduced reality testing, hostility, and antagonism when their grandiose self is threatened (Day, Townsend, & Grenyer, 2020). The malignant narcissist is considered a sociopath or an individual with antisocial behavior, willing to kill a loved person who broke their heart or disobeyed their orders. This personality disorder has severe consequences for the family and society. Such action has been typical of the world's dictators, such as Adolf Hitler (Muller, 2014).

Many clinical studies present that pathological narcissists may express severe depression symptoms and their variability as the depression progresses. Pathological narcissists have symptoms of "empty depression," which results from injuries that a narcissist experienced due to discrepancies between self-perception and the desired self-image (Dawood & Pincus, 2017). The symptoms of such depression are feelings of worthlessness, anhedonia, nihilism, and boredom with life. The researchers state that anhedonia is associated with self-harm and suicidal thoughts. Therefore, pathological narcissists have tendencies to harm themselves and are at high risk of committing suicide. Dawood and Pincus (2017) suggest that taking your own life gives narcissists a sense of control over their life. Research also suggests that depressive disorders are commonly comorbid with NPD.

Normal Narcissism

According to Kiliç and Eryilmaz (2019), the opposite of pathological narcissism is normal narcissism. People with normal narcissism features, in contrast to pathological narcissism, are not as vulnerable to aversive environments, do not have as high self-worth and self-confidence, tend to be fragile, and consider their thoughts as the primary resources states (Kiliç & Eryilmaz, 2019). Muller (2014) has termed normal narcissism "healthy narcissism," which is demonstrated by independent thinking, charisma, passion, risk-taking, alertness, and a sense of humor. The goal of healthy narcissists is to impact and create an external world rather than react to it. Therefore, healthy narcissists often become leaders of nations and various organizations. Ackerman et al. (2011) add that people with normal narcissism features are psychologically healthy and express only some secondary characteristics of a typical narcissist. Such individuals often use strategies to promote a positive self-image; they show adaptive self-enhancement and yearn for success (Ackerman et al., 2011). The healthy form of narcissism may also be a source of positive behavior, such as creativity and a good sense of humor (Peltokangas, 2016). Findings show that these forms of narcissism are categorized as falling in the social rather than the clinical, NPD version of narcissism.

Normal narcissism also supports asserting interpersonal dominance. Such individuals show good adaptive functioning and use their narcissism as motivation to succeed. As presented by Pincus and Lukowitsky (2010), normal narcissists tend to be ambitious, satisfied, and relatively successful. They are also highly addicted to self-esteem, which is responsible for the relation between normal narcissism and good psychological health (Sedikides et al., 2004). Barry and Wallace (2010) have cautioned that the adaptive features of narcissism (e.g., sense of authority and self-sufficiency) do not indicate pathology per se. Still, they may suggest an individual who presents with the sense of power or grandiosity thought to describe a narcissistic individual. Also, adaptive/normal narcissism has not shown the same consistent pattern of association with delinquency or aggression as maladaptive/pathological and tends to correlate with self-esteem positively (Barry & Wallace, 2010).

According to Ronningstam and Baskin-Sommers (2013), pathological narcissism and NPD often coincide in a person. They clashed with consistent or intermittent areas and periods of high functioning, such as areas of real competence and qualities and cognitive, emotional, and interpersonal capabilities, and social skills.

Dark Triad

Machiavellianism

Narcissism falls into the category of Dark Triad; the two other Dark triads are Machiavellianism and psychopathy. According to Paulhus and Williams (2002), Machiavellianism links conceptually to Niccolo Machiavelli's original work, *The Prince*, which is characterized as a guide through deceitful, manipulative leadership practices. The author advised his followers, other leaders, who wanted to become kings, to follow his exact guideline of manipulative, harsh, and deceitful behavior. Machiavelli also explained how to gain and retain political power based solely on expediency while ignoring the traditional values of trust, decency, and honor. However, the author cautioned to use this behavior only when necessary and rule the country with kindness (Kessler et al., 2010). Therefore, researchers claim that Machiavellianism is a multifaceted and incorporates additional attitudes and behaviors beyond deceit or manipulativeness (Kessler et al., 2010; Paulhus and Williams, 2002). The term Machiavellianism had been used predominantly in philosophy and political science; however, scientists noticed similar behavior in leaders in various organizations. Therefore, the term Mach nowadays is also used in social psychology.

In social psychology, Machiavellianism was first studied by Christie and Geis in 1970. The researchers examined whether the traits characteristic for Machiavelli were present among society and used by individuals to manipulate others to achieve their ends at work and daily life (Kessler et al., 2010). The researchers have spotted that individuals with personality traits of Machiavellianism express a lack of concern with conventional morality and low ideological commitment; thus, they are focused on accomplishing a task in the present, rather than thinking of the long term effects of their work (Christie & Geis, 1970). Christie and Geis (1970) designed scales to measure Machiavellianism; Mach IV is a 20-item inventory scored on a 7-point Likert-type scale. The scale is in use to measure Machiavellianism today as well. Machiavellianism has been associated with other psychological constructs, such as paranoia, narcissism, psychopathy, the focus of control, and depression. It has also been associated with more basic dimensions of personality, such as psychoticism, extraversion, and neuroticism (De Hoogh, Den Hartog, & Belschak, 2021).

Specialists have studied Machiavellians (Machs) in terms of their harmful behavior and impact on coworkers in the workplace. It is all due to their tendency to manipulate and exploit others to achieve their personal gain at work. They are strongly goal-driven, focus on what is in their own best interest, and do not shy back from using unethical, counterproductive, and intimidating (leader) behavior to achieve their goals (De Hoogh, Den Hartog, & Belschak, 2021). Evidence from the literature review shows a positive relationship between leader Machiavellianism and abusive supervision, which is described as a sustained display of mistreatment (Christie & Geis, 1970; Kessler et al., 2010). Such behavior has a significant impact on subordinates' well-being. Machiavellians often lie, cheat, and undermine their coworkers and subordinates to reach their own goals and promote themselves as better than anyone else (De Hoogh, Den Hartog, & Belschak, 2021).

The abusive behavior of Machiavellians is a dominant cause of the negative perception of such leaders by their followers. Associates of such individuals claim that their boss is uncaring and lacks genuine concern. In addition, Machs express abusive supervision and hostile behavior toward their followers in the form of verbal and nonverbal abuse (Kiazad et al., 2010). Some of the most common behaviors are being rude, ridiculing a subordinate, and putting him down in front of his colleagues. Generally, they are uncooperative, are devoid of social values, and disregard collective interests, believing that the ends justify the means; therefore, they often engage in the workplace sabotage (Serenko & Choo, 2020).

Researchers have also studied Machiavellians in terms of social exchange theory. Social exchange depends on the quality of the exchange process with the organization. The process includes reliable cooperative alliance with others such as employees meeting their obligations to their leaders, members of teams supporting each other, or leaders being trusted by their subordinates (Molm, 2010). Machiavellians tend to be less successful in meeting demands of social exchange. According to the authors, such behavior is associated with Machs' tendency to break all social norms and rules within the corporate world they exist (Hurley, 2005). The reason for it is Machs' desire to take all the credit and glory for the work done by themselves and others. As a result, Machiavellianism is negatively associated with job performance.

Earlier researchers have mainly focused on the negative impact of Machiavellians on their coworkers and employees; however, they do not always engage in dark behavior. Instead, the recent studies present that Machs successfully follow social norms, act in a friendly manner, and cooperate or contribute to the organization if this is in their best interest (Kessler et al., 2010; Paulhus and Williams, 2002). The reason for it is that Machs disregard moral standards only when it is convenient and only for personal gain. Moreover, Machs appear to be sensitive and responsive to the social context. Den Hartog and Belschak (2012) suggest that Machiavellians show ethical behavior and altruism, but only when it is in their best interest. Those findings indicate that Mach's social behavior depends on the circumstances and situations they are put in.

Machiavellians have the ability to be social chameleons and take on the attitudes and behaviors of those around them, while subtly manipulating the situation to their favor (Hurley, 2005). Thanks to such behavior, Machs can establish powerful social networks and extract desired outcomes from clients. In addition, Machiavellian leaders, due to their chameleon personality, are able to gain the trust and respect of coworkers and increase job performance. Hurley (2005) stated that Machiavellian leaders often engage in a public display of organizational citizenship behaviors motivated by altruistic intentions. Such personas engage in social actions to portray themselves in the best possible light and mask their dark traits. Not to mention, that social engagement of Machs puts the entire organization on the pedestal; thus, the altruistic action supports the society (Hurley, 2005).

Evidence from the research also indicates that Machs are especially sensitive to having autonomy, some latitude, or ambiguity to use more means to achieve their selfish goals. In the low rule climate at work, where the job regulations are bend and company norms and policies are broken by most workers, Machs can expose their abusive behavior; thus, they know they can get away with it. The scenario changes in the high climate organization, where strict rules are in place and are executed (De Hoogh, Den Hartog, & Belschak, 2021). In such situation, it is not easy for Machs to use their tactics, exploit their subordinates, and bend the rules; thus, consequently the organization will reduce and inhibit such behavior (den Hartog and Belschak (2012).

Psychopathy

Psychopathy is the third construct of the Dark Triad of personality disorders. It is also considered the most robust psychological disorder, and individuals suffering from it have a cold, uncaring attitude and minimal empathy toward their coworkers. Lack of empathy often resolves in interpersonal aggression (den Hartog and Belschak (2012). According to De Hoogh, Den Hartog, and Belschak (2021), the term "psychopathy" initially appeared in German psychiatric literature in 1840; however, its symptoms were noticed by the researcher a lot earlier. In the late 19th and early 20th centuries, psychopathy came to the interest of various researchers in criminology, shortly after the psychology and psychiatry research published a seminal book titled *The Mask of Sanity*, which formalized a clinical description of psychopathy (De Hoogh, Den Hartog, & Belschak, 2021).

The most common features of psychopathy include superficial charm, high intelligence, poor judgment, and failure to learn from experience. Such individuals express pathological egocentricity and incapacity for love, making it difficult for a psychopath to engage and keep a loving relationship (Drayton, Santos, & Baskin-Sommers, 2018). Findings suggest that psychopaths fail to consider what others think; therefore, they behave cruel and antisocial ways. However, psychopaths have an intact theory of mind, which means that they can predict what others think and use this ability deliberately to manipulate others' behavior. Such individuals also express a lack of remorse or shame, impulsivity, grandiose sense of self-worth, pathological lying, manipulative behavior, poor self-control, promiscuous sexual behavior, juvenile delinquency, and criminal versatility, among others (Drayton, Santos, & Baskin-Sommers, 2018).

Recent research has classified psychopathy into "organizational" or "corporate construct." This construct aims to distinguish the subclinical or non-pathological form of psychopathy (Landay, Harms, & Credé, 2019). However, both clinical and subclinical approaches generally agree that psychopathy is a constellation of interpersonal, affective, and behavioral personality traits. In addition, psychopathy is composed of three distinct elements that combine to produce the psychopathic personality: boldness (e.g., interpersonal dominance), disinhibition (e.g., impulsivity), and meanness (e.g., lack of empathy: Landay, Harms, & Credé, 2019). Often, on the corporate level, organizations try to assess the level of psychopathy in leadership. Some use the Psychopathic Personality Inventory, which evaluates eight lower-order traits that make up three distinct factors: Fearless Dominance, Self-Centered Impulsivity, and Coldheartedness (Blonigen et al., 2010). However, CEOs often consider this approach inappropriate; therefore, authorities prefer to use the Mischievous (MIS) scale of the Hogan Development Survey (HDS) to assess psychopathic tendencies in the workplace. As mentioned by Landay, Harms, and Credé (2019), the MIS scale itself consists of three subscales labeled Risky (dominant, goal-seeking behaviors), Impulsive (lack of self-control), and Manipulative (willingness to deceive and mistreat others) that reflect the aspects of the triarchic model of psychopathy. The MIS scale is perfect for evaluating the non-clinical population; therefore, it has been used to research problems related to corporate leadership and job performance.

Individuals with psychopathic tendencies possess a number of personality characteristics that determine their success at the workplace. Some of the traits may not be considered negative when considering leadership emergence and leadership effectiveness (Landay, Harms, & Credé, 2019). Leadership emergence is associated with a person's ability to become a leader in a group or a team (Grijalva et al., 2015). Leadership effectiveness relates to team effectiveness and job performance or perceptions of whether the leader is effective (Harms, Spain, & Hannah, 2011; Nevicka et al., 2018). Research indicates that psychopathic tendencies have been found to predict corporate rank, both positively and negatively positively. Yet it all depends on hierarchical position or time to promotion (Harms, Spain, & Hannah, 2011).

Evidence shows that psychopathic tendencies with leadership effectiveness are also mixed. Good and effective leaders are seen amongst some American presidents. As Lilienfeld et al. (2012) say, U.S. presidents have a positive link between aspects of psychopathy and political effectiveness. Nevertheless, it has been proven that although some individuals with psychopathic personality are perceived as good and effective leaders, the majority is considered to have a negative impact on followers and result in abusive supervision (Mathieu & Babiak, 2016). The effectiveness of a psychopathic leader can be measured in various ways. Landay, Harms, and Credé (2019) states that leadership effectiveness might be objective (e.g., firm financial performance) or subjective (e.g., ratings of leadership performance). Leadership performance can be measured by self-ratings, supervisor ratings, or followers rating their own outcomes as affected by their leader.

Regardless of the type of psychopathic leader effectiveness measurements, such individuals' behavior greatly impacts the performance of their immediate workers. Boddy (2014) claims that psychopathic tendencies in leadership result in a negative impact on followers' outcomes. Bullying, abusive supervision, low job satisfaction, and employee turnover intentions are the most common negative outcomes. The abusive supervision is expressed in hostile verbal and nonverbal behaviors, indifference, and rudeness (Boddy, 2014). Babiak and Hare (2006) concluded that corporate psychopathy also results in difficulty in forming a team, sharing ideas and credit with others, and the inability to make an effective transition following a promotion. In addition, psychopathic leaders show disparate treatment of staff, deceptiveness, immodesty, inability to accept blame. Such individuals often act unpredictably, impulsively, or aggressively (Babiak & Hare, 2006).

The behavior of a psychopathic leader has a terrible impact on the work atmosphere among teams led by such individual. Babiak and Hare (2006) stated that some psychopathic leaders' behavior leads to career "derailment": poor interpersonal skills (i.e., being arrogant, cold, insensitive, and overly ambitious). It is related to their controlling and unsupportive management style, which doesn't provide supportive feedback, or fails to clarify responsibilities. In addition, employees experience problems completing tasks and getting work done because they have little trust in their leadership, who has difficulties following through with their promises (Webster & Smith, 2018).

Psychopathic leaders prefer autonomy and exhibit a lack of concern for authoritative structures. Therefore, the best scenario for such individuals in a workplace is a position where they can have independence and complete decision making, hence their desire to hold higher status (Webster & Smith, 2018). Only in this instance a psychopathic employee can thrive and bring positive outcomes to the company and the coworkers. In addition, leaders high on psychopathy are very protective of their careers; therefore, arranging an environment with room for improvement of work-related knowledge and skills is essential.

Individuals high on psychopathy can have a positive impact on organizational outcomes. Such leaders are politically astute and can exhibit strong communication skills in social settings. It has been noticed by Webster and colleagues (2018) that psychopaths are keen on relatedness and help to co-workers only when they see social and political advantages for themselves. Therefore, it could be viewed as an excellent motivational technique to encourage leaders with the psychopathic personality to be more proactive and engage in teamwork (Webster & Smith, 2018).

In the social work construct, psychopaths are career-focused; therefore, they excel as leaders in the leadership emergence stage during the recruitment process and promotions. Psychopaths use their superficial charisma and calculative approach to career advancement to charm their leaders (De Hoogh, Den Hartog, & Belschak, 2021). Leaders with psychopathic dispositions quickly gain their employees' trust due to their insincere altruism and fake charm. Sometimes they offer valuable knowledge and promise to help workers grow, when in fact, they wait for a perfect moment to unleash their dark side and devaluate followers (Drayton, Santos, & Baskin-Sommers, 2018).

Narcissism vs. Prototypical Leader Traits

The other aspect presented in the previous literature and essential for the upcoming subject is the link between narcissistic personality traits and prototypical leader traits. The existing literature has mentioned this correlation; thus, many individuals with narcissistic personality traits also demonstrate leadership qualities in an organization. Czarna and Nevicka (2019) have noted that grandiose narcissism is more correlated with leadership and prototypical leader traits than vulnerable narcissism is. The authors have also noticed that narcissistic leaders often fit perfectly into people's leadership schemas of prototypical leadership traits (Czarna & Nevicka, 2019). Some of the core narcissistic characteristics fit perfectly into the concept of prototypical leadership. Researchers have determined that the prototypical leader's main features are confidence, dominance, and extraversion (Foti et al., 2012; Judge, LePine, & Rich, 2015; Keller Hansbrough & Jones, 2014; Nevicka et al., 2018). These features are also typical of grandiose narcissists. Galvin, Lange, and Ashforth (2014) suggested that when in contact with other people, especially followers, leaders with prototypical traits are very charming, enthusiastic, and humorous in their verbal expressions. Such behaviors have caught people's attention and made the leader attractive to followers. Those features are especially useful in contact with clients.

Brunell and colleagues (2008) looked at the problem of narcissistic leader traits from the perspective of leader emergence. In their study, the authors stated that narcissists are considered good leader material due to their desire for power and social status. Such individuals use their strong features and desires to achieve their goals, and in this instance, it is to be a leader (Brunell et al., 2008). In addition, narcissists are great at forming new relationships with people. They are great at initiating romantic relationships and engaging in early-stage interaction with strangers, which can be used as an asset when speaking to new clients. With their humorous approach, narcissists are perceived as easy going and fun to be around people. Those features are desired amongst the leaders of an organization; thus, they assure good relations with possible clients (Brunell et al., 2008). However, as Brunell and colleagues (2008) noticed, those attributes of narcissists are only beneficial in the leader emergence stage. They tend to fade out as the narcissist reveals more of his negative traits.

Hoffman, Helland, and Blair (2008) discovered that narcissists often nominate themselves for challenging tasks, which is a positive attribute of an effective leader. Such people engage in harder work when they see an opportunity for reward or glory. It is all related to their desire for power and need to be at the top. Those leaders are also known to motivate their subordinates and coworkers to work harder so they achieve success quicker (Hoffman, Helland, & Blair, 2008). Those attributes are very desirable amongst leaders, especially if they are about to leader a large group of people or organization. The next feature that is associated with narcissism and leadership is the grand vision and ability to inspire others. Also, Rosenthal and Pittinsky (2006) have noticed that some specific characteristics, such as dominance and supreme confidence of narcissists, are inspiring to followers. These are precisely the features that people look for in a leader. They want to be guided by a vibrant and energetic persona who can lead them through their employment process.

Szabó and Jones (2019) examined that narcissistic leaders, along with Machiavellians and some psychopaths, are often considered mentally tough and resilient due to their strategic and flexible thinking. The authors used the Clough, Earle, and Sewell (2002) 4c methods to define mental toughness. The method is made of four elements: commitment (i.e., deep involvement in pursuits and activities despite difficulties that arise), control (i.e., the tendency to feel and act as if one is influential in determining outcomes and keep anxieties in check), challenge (i.e., the degree to which individuals view difficulties as personal development opportunities), and confidence (i.e., a high sense of self-belief concerning one's ability to cope with setbacks and to achieve success; Clough, Earle, & Sewell, 2002). As mentioned in the study, mentally tough individuals can keep adversarial or challenging situations under control, which prevents negative effects of stress and is often associated with positive outcomes in achievement-related contexts.

Maccoby (2014) describes leaders as visionaries and innovators who shape the future of the organization they lead. This makes productive leaders. The vision site of their character allows them to see the big picture, which, along the way, leads them to glory and power. As Maccoby (2014) has noticed, such individuals leave the analyzing and actual job to their workers. Maccoby (2014) also mentions narcissist's ability to inspire significant numbers of followers, who are amazed by the charisma and vision of narcissists. In return, the narcissists gain a "free" workforce and admiration and conviction of their vision. The attributes presented by Maccoby are also assigned to the great leaders of big organizations.

Also, as examined by Nevicka et al. (2013), people with prototypical leader traits are not static and easily adjust to situations. The exceptional energy and charisma of these leaders are typical behaviors of grandiose narcissists (Sedikides & Campbell, 2017). Experts have also added that having a bold vision, enthusiasm when pitching ideas, and persistence during obstacles are traits that narcissists and prototypical leaders have in common (Nevicka et al., 2013). Thus, they are traits that are not only possessed by narcissists but also desired in leaders, as they allow leaders to run organizations successfully. Although the concept of a prototypical leader does feature positive personality traits, studies have shown that such people also have negative characteristics such as arrogance, lack of empathy, exploitativeness, and manipulativeness (Miller et al., 2012; Nevicka et al., 2013; Sedikides & Campbell, 2017). This information has provided useful insights for future research as it has shown that narcissists could be successful leaders in organizations because their personality features are similar to those of a prototypical leader. From a scientific perspective, such people may seem to fit these responsible positions well because they can withstand stress and complicated situations and are socially skilled in leading people.

Narcissistic Leader and the Abuse of Power

In the literature review about narcissistic leaders, a significant section is devoted to the dark side of the narcissistic boss and his abuse of power. The authors of various articles have given this phenomenon multiple names: leadership derailment, toxic leadership, destructive leadership, abusive leadership, negative leadership, or the evil leadership style. However, regardless of the name assigned to this leadership style, it all comes down to the same agenda: the prevalence of narcissist traits in each description (Camm, 2014).

It has been said earlier that narcissistic leaders possess many characteristics recognized by society as positive prototypical leader traits. The most prominent ones are extraversion, willingness to take risks, charisma as well as grand vision. Those visionaries often rise to high positions as leaders in organizations. Such individuals are admired as transformational leaders because, inspired by their vision, they bring a lot of valuable changes to their workplace (O'Reilly & Chatman, 2020). Narcissistic leaders are skillful orators and persuasive personalities. They crave attention, which makes them perfect follower's gatherers. In addition, narcissistic bosses express the perseverance to follow a vision despite their subordinates' resistance (Camm, 2014). O'Reilly and Chatman (2020) speak about famous personas such Steve Jobs (founder of Apple), Adam Newman (founder of WeWork), and Travis Kalanik (founder of Uber) as great examples of business owners with a grand vision who made their business grow significantly. In spite of their tremendous work and achievements, there is also a dark side of their character that is known only by those who work closely with the narcissistic individuals. Some narcissistic leaders indeed let their darker side take over the features of their character, which as a result leads to the abuse of power. The abuse of power among narcissistic leaders in organizations is a widespread occurrence often drastic in consequences for the employees and the organization.

The abuse of power is strictly associated with basic traits of NPD, the pathological form of narcissism. In their research, Kacel, Ennis and Pereira (2017) state that NPD is "characterized by a persistent pattern of grandiosity, fantasies of unlimited power or importance, and the need for admiration or special treatment." In other words, the individuals with the signs of clinical version of narcissism seek power in every aspect of their life. Such behavior is also carried out to the work environment. Therefore, narcissists always peruse the leadership positions at work for their personal interest of gaining power over other employees (Asrar-ul-Hag & Anjum, 2020).

To prove the matter, the scientists performed numerous studies examining the relation between narcissism and leaders' abuse of power. Rovelli and Curnis (2020) mention in their research that those who show five narcissistic personality traits climb the corporate ladder much faster than their peers. The study is based on interviews among the 172 Italian CEOs who tested for narcissistic personality traits. For this case, the researchers used the NPD inventory test. The results have shown that those who scored higher on the five main features of NPD: extraversion, overconfidence, self-esteem, dominance, and authoritarianism were more likely to get appointed CEO after a certain amount of time at their firm. The ratio came to 29% higher in oppose to individuals who scored low on narcissistic features.

Toxic Triangle

The researchers have also concluded that toxic leadership does not happen overnight. For a leader to become toxic, he has to possess narcissistic personality traits or other dark and destructive personality traits. In addition, there have to be susceptible followers and the contributing environment in which they interact (Singh, Sengupta, & Dev, 2018). Such occurrence is called the Toxic Triangle. The interaction of the components of a toxic triangle determine the intensity of toxic leadership and the abuse of power in the work place. The first and the main component of this triangle is the destructive leader. Padilla, Hogan, and Kaiser (2007) assign five personality features that an individual should possess to meet the criteria: charisma, narcissism, personalized power, the ideology of hate, and negative life themes. The abuse of power also happens where there are employees responsive to the toxic behavior of their leader. The author has verified two types of such subordinates: the conformers and colluders. Conformers express low maturity, low core self-evaluation, and unmet needs, which means that their boss will easily manipulate them. Conformers adhere to such leaders to avoid incongruities for risk of reprisal (Padilla, Hogan, & Kaiser, 2007). The colluders have traits similar to destructive leaders. They are ambitious, have the same world views, and follow the same bad values; therefore, they happily follow their leader. Padilla, Hogan, and Kaiser (2007) have also noticed that the emergence of abusive leaders is also a result of the need for narcissistic individuals to protect their power, status, and control over their employees. The corporate environment is often considered the incubator for the abusive leaders, due to excessive internal competition, counterproductive policies and practices with unreasonable goals, and cultures that encourage blame game (Singh, Sengupta, & Dev, 2018).

Despite the toxic triangle, which creates a perfect environment for the abuse of power, there have been other possible causes recognized as the reason for destructive leadership. The most common ones are incompetence, rigid attitude, corruption, lack of corporate control measures, and toxic culture at the workplace. Rovelli and Curnis (2020) stated that the immense scope of the abuse of power is indicated by narcissistic personality traits, which are often acquired through childhood. However, evidence from the authors' research says that some Italian CEOs attain narcissistic personality traits after gaining power in a business (Rovelli & Curnis, 2020). The sense of power gives them the ability to control the corporate environment: resources, rewards, and punishments, which makes them feel in control and encourages executing narcissistic behavior. Denis Tourish (2013) also noticed the impact that power has on people possessing it. Tourish (2013) states that "power adversely affects peoples' ethics, perception of others, testosterone level, and inclination to engage in risky behavior." The author also mentions that people are sensitive to the presence or lack of power in nature, which indicates that once they obtain it, they guard it with all means. Hitesh Bhasin (2019) also adds to the conversation that power comes with authority. It means that once an individual reaches a certain level in the company's hierarchy he gains power. Adversely as the power percolates down the hierarchy, it reduces. All in all, abusive behavior is associated with the narcissistic personality of the abuser and his desire for power.

Examples of Abuse of Power

The abuse of power executed by the narcissistic leader in the workplace is usually seen as using one's capabilities outside the usual scope of action or extending their rights beyond their job description. An individual can exercise the abuse of power physically or verbally. In some cases, toxic leaders use psychological abuse to stay within the legal lane of action (Bhasin, 2019). The authority is often misused toward the lower-level employees. It occurs in destructive behavior such as being critical and aggressive toward lower-level subordinates and using employees as tools while blaming them for your lack of knowledge. The other forms of abuse of power are micromanagement and jealousy over those who have advanced levels of critical thinking (Singh, Sengupta, & Dev, 2018). Researchers also noticed that narcissistic leaders make unreasonable demands toward their subordinates and are intolerable to others' views (Rovelli & Curnis, 2020; Tourish, 2013), yet another form of abuse. Ana Teresa Verdasca (2011) states in her research that the perpetrator exercises its power to restrict the victim's behavior, affecting its position and even his integrity. The author says that there is a strict dependency issue, in which the narcissistic leader controls the resources that the victim needs, making him vulnerable to narcissistic perpetrator demands.

Verdasca (2011) distinguishes five sources of power: Coercive, Legitimate, Reward, Expert, and Referent. Each type of power held by the narcissistic leader is devastating in results toward the subordinates. The author claims that "coercive power is exercised through punitive sanctions: the power to dismiss, the power to act disciplinarily against an employee. In some cases and subordinates may be excluded from the social group" (Verdasca, 2011). Legitimate power is obtained through the company policy and growth as an individual within the corporate structures. Legitimate power is associated with authority and respect. Hence, in the hands of a narcissistic individual, it may become a tool of destruction. The Rewarding and Punishing power is a part of an appointed leadership role. However, toxic leaders make appointed tasks unreasonable or impossible targets or deadlines. Employees receive unmanageable workloads, and their work is excessively monitored. As per rewards, the superior may refrain from assigning an employee for a raise or advancement at work (Verdasca, 2011). Lastly, there is the Expert and Referent power. Expert power occurs when a narcissistic individual possesses control over important information or resources. In this instance, the abuser of authority happens when a leader withholds that valuable information, making the subordinate's work much more challenging to complete. The Referent power is linked with an individual who is admired and respected in the workplace. The abuse of power happens when such individuals ignore some team members, exclude them from social events, or spread wrongful gossip about them (Verdasca, 2011). The literature review shows that regardless of the source of the abuse of power, a narcissistic leader's hands can be devastating to his follower and the entire organization as well.

Corporate Narcissism and Gender Differences

It is also worth investigating the gender aspect of narcissistic leaders in organizations. It is because many more women hold higher positions within the corporate world and might have narcissistic personalities. There is very little research done that treats the subject of gender differences in corporate narcissism. However, there are indications that men are more narcissistic than are women. The prevalence of lifetime NPD is greater for men (7.7%) than it is for women (4.8%), according to results from the *National Epidemiological Survey on Alcohol and Related Conditions* (Stinson et al., 2008). In the past, Freud claimed that women were more narcissistic than men; thus, he believed women were more preoccupied with their appearance and used to make choices regarding their "self" (Grijalva et al., 2013). It means, according to Freud, that women were more self-centered. However, social norms and gender stereotypes, based on gender labor division, show that gender in narcissism is more related to the social expectation given to each man and woman. Research presented by Roberts and Robins (2000) that society expects men to be career-oriented, possess leadership ability, and be aggressive, assertive, and independent. In contrast, men's most undesirable traits (proscriptive traits) included emotional, naïve, weak, insecure, and gullible. The pressure and high expectations may lead to paternal and demanding leadership style development. Following the above thought process men were dominant, because socially dominance was reserved for men.

On the contrary, women were expected to be emotional, warm, interested in children, sensitive to others, and good listeners. In contrast, women's most undesirable (proscriptive) traits included aggressive, intimidating, dominating, arrogant, and rebellious (Grijalva et al., 2013). Moreover, women had harsher sanctions for displaying features characteristic of the dominant and narcissistic person (De Hoogh, Hartog, & Nevicka, 2015). Therefore, in the past, narcissistic behavior was reserved only for men. Such understanding of social roles and acceptance of stereotypes lets us believe that negative perception of women when they display an assertive, directive leadership style, penalties for women who desire power, and punishments for women who exhibit high levels of self-promotion. Hence, stereotypes of social gender differences create societal pressure for women, more so than for men, to suppress displays of narcissism. It could be the case why, in the past, there were more narcissistic male leaders in opposed to narcissistic female leaders (De Hoogh, Hartog, & Nevicka, 2015).

The significant impact on gender differences in narcissistic corporate leaders is caused by cultural patriarchy and women occupying lower status positions. Researchers in Western culture noticed that shift in the job market has changed, and more women are entering positions solely reserved for men, including leadership and managerial jobs. According to the U.S. Bureau of Labor Statistic (2020), women now make up 46.9% of the U.S. labor market vs. 30% in 1950 (U.S. Bureau of Labor Statistic, 2020). Thus, as the times and gender roles decrease, women entering higher positions might have narcissistic personalities. However, the research shows significant differences in narcissistic leaders considering gender (Grijalva et al., 2013). The latest study focuses on gender differences in the facets of the Narcissistic Personality Inventory (NPI), including Exploitative/Entitlement (E/E), Leadership/Authority (L/A), and Grandiose/Exhibitionism (G/E).

E/E is associated with toxic behaviors such as aggression, counterproductive work behavior (CWB) (e.g., theft, sharing confidential company information), and harassing coworkers. As mentioned earlier, women are generally penalized for such behavior; therefore, they refrained from expressing aggression toward their coworkers and subordinates. At the same time, men exhibit higher levels of E/E than do women (Grijalva et al., 2013). It has also been noted by O'Brien et al. (2012) that men's sense of personal entitlement concerning pay is higher than are women's. In addition, men are, for some reason, more deserving than women, entitled to more resources than are women.

The L/A is associated with an individual's desire for power and authority. In gender differences concerning L/A, men are more motivated to obtain leadership roles. It is also related to genders stereotypes, where leader stereotypes are linked with agency and masculinity (O'Brien et al., 2012). Lastly, the G/E facet measures vanity, self-absorption, superiority, and exhibitionistic tendencies (Ackerman et al., 2011). Historically speaking, women for generations were raised to be preoccupied with their own physical appearance in opposed to men. Therefore, it is probable that women may score high on the G/E scale. On the contrary, many men score high on other G/E items, such as those reflecting self-absorption (e.g., "I really like to be the center of attention," Ackerman et al., 2011). It means that there are no fundamental gender differences in the G/E construct of narcissism. Although women gained more social rights over the decades, entered the job market, and presented more desire for power and authority, there are no significant changes in the gender difference in narcissism that there were before. There is still a considerable disparity between narcissistic female leaders in opposed to narcissistic male leaders.

The gender differences among narcissistic leaders were also measured in the context of the Leader-Member Exchange model (LMX). The study was performed in the accounting profession in the United States. The findings show that there is a significant difference in the perception between genders regarding how LMX mediates between narcissistic leadership and employee job satisfaction in the accounting profession (Shurden,

2018). While under the supervision of narcissistic male leaders, employees' lower job satisfaction is related to the managerial effectiveness of such individuals, which is strongly determined by one's ability to influence others, whether they be subordinates or superiors, or even peers. However, it all comes at a great employee expense; thus, men are more direct and to the point. Male leaders also have a commanding physical presence and display "power" (Shurden, 2018). Considering the difference in leadership styles, men can be too blunt and direct, often too confident in their opinion. They also are not empathetic enough and are often insensitive, making employees have difficulties communicating with their managers.

Recent findings also show that narcissistic female leaders use slightly different management styles while guiding their employees. In the context of LMX, female leaders use a more communicative approach and empathy in guiding their employees. This leadership style plays a significant role in how women as leaders are perceived regarding their leadership role in the organization instead of the same position held by their male colleagues (Goman, 2016). Furthermore, Ackerman et al. (2011) mentioned that women are better listeners, more empathetic, and better at dialogue. In addition, they are the ability to read language and the ability to detect nonverbal cues. Although those are strong features expected from a good leader, they can be perceived as weakness; thus, women can be too emotional, often won't get to the point in a conversation, and are not authoritative enough. Shurden (2018) also noticed that gender of employees is a significant element in determining the perception of narcissistic leaders in the organization. The researchers claim that male workers are more troubled by having a narcissistic leader than are females because women value a strong leader (Shurden, 2018). In contrast, male employees treat such an individual as a threat and competition. Authors have also noticed that female employees communicate less often difficulties at work when men are more outspoken and vocal if they are dissatisfied with their job.

Why People Follow Narcissistic Leaders

It has been also noticed during the literature review that although the abuse of power exercised by narcissistic leaders is drastic in consequences to their subordinates, many of the employees follow their narcissistic bosses. Beth Ellwood (2021) states in her article that narcissistic individuals tend to faster reach heights of their managerial career than the less narcissistic candidates. The main reason for it is narcissistic traits of their personality such as authoritarianism, higher ambition, and greater confidence, which make people follow those individuals. The ambition and grand vision is also considered as a valuable trait because leaders who think alike achieve great success in creating the strategy of the firms they run, as well as for the management of operations, and mobilization of resources, which ultimately impact financial performance. Subordinates look up to people who are considered a god-like figure; thus, they can learn and use their managing techniques in their own future career (Ellwood, 2021). It has also been noticed that employees create and the illusion of narcissistic leaders as heroes. They also consider themselves the chosen ones, appointed by the leaders to perform unique tasks or participate in better projects. It is, therefore, only the illusion of a great leader; however, it attracts subordinates who set high goals for themselves.

Working closely with a narcissistic leader gives the opportunity to be a part of big projects in the company. The more an employee can work hand in hand with your boss, the more chances there are to be in the center of the action. Such workers hope to get some of the glory for accomplishing complex tasks and possibly some rewards, especially if the project is a big success for the firm. It is essential to notice that narcissists dislike sharing the glory with others and tend to assign the accomplishments of others to themselves (Ellwood, 2021). Researchers have found that the psychological reason behind the following narcissistic leader is associated with humans' need for immortality and legacy and last symbolically forever. In this instance, they hope that they will accomplish success by following a successful persona, and memorable things will be engraved in their name in history (Conger & Kanungo, 2016). Unfortunately, while working with toxic leaders, there are very few chances that an employee will have outstanding achievements accounted for in their work history. So it all comes to narcissists' need to be the best regardless of the means necessary for it. In addition, there is a faulty understanding from employees that narcissist as a divine persona will care for his workers and followers. Conger and Kanungo (2016) state in their study that narcissistic leaders tend to present a bold vision of the future, and this makes them more charismatic in the eyes of others. Subordinates feel that such a charismatic leader can empower them with proper motivation and reward program. However, it has been shown by the researchers that it is only a temporary event, thus toxic leaders only care for themselves and their own success and work (Conger & Kanungo, 2016). Narcissistic individuals radiate "an image of a prototypically effective leader." Narcissistic leaders know how to draw attention toward themselves because they enjoy the visibility. It takes time for employees to see that these early signals of competence are not later realized, and that a leader's narcissism reduces the exchange of information among team members and often negatively affects group performance.

Discussion

As the literature review showed, experts have identified various types of narcissists, and this study focuses on grandiose and vulnerable ones (Carter & Douglass, 2018; Jauk et al., 2017) and normal and pathological ones (Ackerman et al., 2011; Kiliç & Eryilmaz, 2019; Muller et al., 2014). They base on the same core features of narcissism but vary slightly when it comes to some detailed characteristics. Researchers have provided evidence that such division is necessary to link narcissism with leadership and prototypical leadership traits (Czarna & Nevicka, 2019). Furthermore, experts have also pointed out that the grandiose form of narcissism has stronger ties to leadership characteristics as opposed to the vulnerable type. As presented by experts, grandiose narcissists possess a good sense of leadership, which makes them excellent leaders (Giacomin, 2016). It has all been due to their charisma, confidence, and visionary communication skills (Zajenkowski et al., 2018). Experts have also noted that vulnerable narcissists tend to fall into depression and anxiety (Campbell et al., 2011), which indicates that they could experience difficulties when managing people. The evidence also has shown that their antisocial, hostile, and passive-aggressive behaviors suggest that they would rather keep people away than lead them (Rogoza et al., 2018).

Some researchers have focused their studies on developing a proper definition of narcissism, which could help readers categorize and understand such personality traits. Muller (2014), as one of the few who has done this, focused his work solely on describing a narcissist. He divided narcissism into healthy narcissism, pathological narcissism, MN, and narcissism as a psychological disorder (that is, NPD). Ackerman et al. (2011) have added that a person with NPD possesses features, such as the need for admiration, a sense of grandiosity, and a lack of empathy, which escalate with time and eventually lead to dysfunctional behaviors. Such behaviors are not ones that leaders should have; thus, it is essential to know the differences between healthy narcissism and the clinical version, NPD. Kiliç and Eryilmaz (2019) have stated that individuals with NPD put their needs on the pedestal, so they crush emotionally when these needs are not met. Such trait has also not been recommended among leaders. This information thus constitutes evidence that not all narcissists should be leaders.

Methods of Leader Evaluation

This research's interest has been narcissism at the leadership level and forms of narcissistic leader evaluation within a given organization. The assessment of narcissistic leaders influences how subordinates perceive narcissistic leaders and the outcome of such a leader in the organization. Therefore, the evaluation of leaders has been divided into two main categories: the assessment of narcissistic personality traits and leader evaluation. Thus far, researchers have used various methods to evaluate narcissistic leaders. The most common methods are the NPI by Raskin and Terry (1988), NPI-16 by Ames, Rose, and Anderson (2006), the California Psychological Inventory (CPI) by Wink and Gough (1990), the HDS – termed "BOLD" – by Hogan and Hogan (2009), and Chatterjee and Hambrick (2007) and many others' method, which includes measuring the number of photographs of the CEO in annual reports and press releases, the use of first-person singular pronouns in interviews, and the compensation relative to the second-highest–paid executive. Leaders can also be evaluated twice in the organization, first through a self-assessment and then through an assessment done by others. This study's main focus is the two major types of leader assessment – self-reports (self-evaluation) and others' reports (others' evaluations or assessments) – as the factor influencing the overall perception of narcissistic leaders in organizations.

Assessment of Narcissism

In various significant studies on narcissism, researchers have used the social-personality psychology inventory to test the level of narcissism in individuals, as have organizations that needed to measure narcissism in leaders. In the reviewed research, leaders' narcissism has been tested using the NPI (Raskin & Terry, 1988). The first version of NPI is based on NPD, and it was expected to be included in the DSM-III (Ackerman et al., 2011). The NPI has been the most common instrument used to measure narcissism in people and has been considered a useful way to determine whether someone has grandiose narcissism. The test measures subclinical narcissism; therefore, it does not indicate whether a person has NPD (Germain, 2017). It measures various personality dimensions, such as exploitativeness/entitlement and leadership/ authority (Ackerman et al., 2011). It has been said by Germain (2017) that individuals who score high on the exploitativeness/entitlement dimension express features of self-consciousness, low levels of social desirability, and empathy as well as lower self-esteem. However, people with high L/A scores show higher self-awareness and self-esteem, lower social anxiety, personal distress, and depression (Ackerman et al., 2011). Such a form of narcissism has been called adaptive or adaptive self-functioning narcissism.

The NPI is a set of 40 questions composed of pairs of items, in which one item is considered narcissistic and the other non-narcissistic (Kubarych, Deary, & Austin, 2003). It is a relatively lengthy procedure; therefore, some researchers or departments in organizations alter the NPI questions to the most applicable for their organizational settings. The advantage of this test is that it can be altered to fit a given study's or organization's needs. Galvin, Waldman, and Balthazard (2010) modified the NPI scale to fit the needs of their study by eliminating questions concerning leaders' looks, such as "I like to look at my body" or "I like to start new fads of fashion" (p. 519). These types of questions were created for college students and, therefore, are inappropriate for high-level managers or leaders. In their research on the perception of narcissism, Ong et al. (2016) also used the NPI scale to measure the rate of narcissism among students. However, for their study's purpose, they removed the questions concerning narcissism to avoid indication of narcissism in specific individuals. Although it is often modified, NPI has been the standard most-used procedure to measure narcissism and leadership predispositions among individuals in organizations.

The other standard method of evaluating narcissistic individuals in organizations is the NPI-16 by Ames, Rose, and Anderson (2006). It was created as a shortened version of the NPI, and its items were created as face validity as an indicator of narcissism (Bierhoff, Margraf, & Brailovskaia, 2019). Ames, Rose, and Anderson (2006) designed and compared the NPI-16 to the NPI-40 (the extended version of the narcissism scale) and concluded that the NPI-16 is equally valid and well-adjusted to companies where the extended version seems impractical. The NPI-16 is composed of 16 pairs of questions extracted from the NPI-40 and specifically oriented toward narcissism measurements (Germain, 2017). This narcissism assessment method has been used in situations where there is not much time and a quick evaluation was needed and well-suited for workplaces (Campbell et al., 2011).

Harrison Gough invented a test to measure behavior patterns, interpersonal style, and personality traits within society (Harrison et al., 2017). According to Gough, the assessment was supposed to be universal; therefore, one of the scales has been a folk scale (Stewart, 2008). His test, the CPI, is cross-culturally relevant, straight-forward, and easy to interpret. The test can also describe behavior patterns and predict the behavior of specific individuals. Researchers and practitioners have used the CPI to assess people in counseling, education, psychology, and various industries and organizations (Megargee, 2009). The CPI can also be used to evaluate particular personality traits, which can be linked with leadership and corporate work, such as managerial potential, work orientation, leadership, and narcissism (Megargee, 2009). Stewart (2008) stated that CPI is used best to identify talents and highlight weaknesses and strengths among an organization's employees. The test has often been administered to young individuals to assess their leadership development in the pre-employment process (Stewart, 2008). Therefore, researchers such as Blair, Hoffman, and Helland (2008), Hoffman, Helland, and Blair (2008) used the CPI scale as a form of self-assessment to measure narcissism among their study's participants.

It has also been noticed that human resource specialists from organizations often use the HDS as a form of personality evaluation among their employees. Initially, the survey was created as a paper version by Hogan, but currently, the survey is available in an electronic version and has been translated into 32 languages (Harms, 2017). It is an extensive measure of subclinical personality detailers. The survey is not used for clinical purposes, although it consists of 11 scales that align with the DSM-IV Axis II personality disorders (Harms, 2017). There has been created the Bold version of HDS exists, and it contains 14 items as part of an extended version of the personality test that can determine narcissism in leaders (Germain, 2017). The Bold version of the test has fallen into the category of mirroring neurotic tendencies such as "move against," "move towards," and "move away" (Harms, 2017, p. 1). The HDS measures personality characteristics that can be linked with antisocial personality and psychopathy (Adams, 2015). The HDS Bold has been used to define narcissism in non-pathological environments by applying self-reporting tools. It has been said by Adams (2015) that HDS Bold is a useful tool that can help in the selection of a good leader; thus, it helps select narcissistic and psychopathic personality traits. Adam has suggested that personality inventories could be used to determine the negative attributes of narcissistic people because narcissistic leaders deceive others with their intelligence and charm (Adams, 2015).

Researchers have also supported the method of evaluating narcissism called the "prominence of the CEO photograph in the annual report" and ideated by Chatterjee and Hambrick (Germain, 2017). This method has mainly been used to test narcissism among CEOs and high-level directors of organizations because they are often. The reason for it has been that directors and CEOs of major organizations were unwilling to fill out self-report surveys on narcissism (Olsen, Dworkis, & Young, 2014). Thus, Chatterjee and Hambrick have created an unobtrusive method to determine narcissism in leaders. Perez (2017) has stated that those measures are observable indicators aligned with four NPI elements, such as the CEO's photograph's prominence in the annual report. In this method, the researchers assumed that the photographs and yearly reports are controlled by the CEO and are often used by the CEO to showcase themselves, thus demonstrating their sense of entitlement and self-absorption (Perez, 2017). Chatterjee and Hambrick (2007) used conceptual elements to develop this narcissism index. The index consists of items concerning self-absorption/self-admiration, L/A, and exploitativeness/entitlement.

The method of using the CEO photographs' prominence in the annual report has been sometimes altered to fit a given organization's expectations. Olsen, Dworkis, and Young (2014) added features of relative cash and non-cash pay to the second-highest paid executive and the size and composition of the photograph to compare the CEO's narcissism and accounting. Perez (2017) claimed that the prominence of photographs of the CEO may not be a reliable measurement of narcissism; for example, the company may desire to showcase the CEO to promote the firm, and thus, having many pictures of the CEO is part of a company's intended and deliberate marketing strategy. Therefore, this measure of narcissism in leaders or CEOs is often supported by other methods such as the NPI (Olsen, Dworkis, & Young, 2014).

There is also a Dark Triad narcissism scale constructed by Jones and Paulhus (2014). It accounts for the traits of dark personalities such as psychopathy and Machiavellianism as well as narcissism. In some cases, authors also use this scale for testing people who express everyday sadism, sensational interests, and moralism (Jones & Paulhus, 2014). Primary, the Dark Triad was composed of three independent constructs with some overlap. It contains 91 items questionnaire on dark personality traits. The complexity of this scale, as well as the time needed to complete it, has been the significant disadvantage of this assessment method. Therefore, researchers rarely use it. However, it did help to evaluate the level of narcissism among narcissistic leaders in organizations.

Dirty Dozen (DD) is yet another form of testing narcissism in individuals. Jonason and Webster created the test in 2010. The test is a 12-item questionnaire composed of 4 sections containing the Dark Triad personality characteristics such as psychopathy, narcissism, and Machiavellianism. The responses to the questions are rated up to 7-point Likert chart. In this instance, 1 is strong disagreement, and 7 is the opposite (Braun, 2017). The instrument was primary used to test dark traits among the subclinical individuals. In the aspect of Machiavellianism, the scale measures the deceitfulness, manipulativeness, and likelihood of exploitation for personal gain. In the range of psychopathy, the instrument assesses callousness, amorality, lack of remorse, and cynicism. Lastly, it measures if an individual seeks attention, admiration, status, and if such a person needs favors from others in terms of narcissism. This method has been used to predict risky behavior. The authors of this scale concluded that triad individuals express converge on specific voluntary adaptation, which is the impulsive and short-term mating strategy (Braun, 2017).

The other measurement scale of narcissism used by researchers is the Supernumerary Personality Inventory – Egotism Scale created by Paunonem (SPI, Braun, 2017). The scale is composed of 150 statements to be rated on 5-point scales. Anchors are: strongly disagree (1) and strongly agree (5) on the Likert chart (Braun, 2017). The scale's main focus was to measure the ten facet-level traits such as manipulativeness, conventionality, humorousness, seductiveness,

Others' Reports

Others' reports are a form of leader evaluation performed in an organization to measure the level of narcissism in leaders and the opinion that other people have of a given leader. Various researchers have also termed others' reports as peer assessments, subordinate reports, or others' evaluations (Galvin, Waldman, & Balthazard, 2010). The primary purpose of using subordinate reports of leaders is to eliminate self-assessment and biased opinions or perceptions of oneself. Others' ratings may have various forms, depending on the organization and the results they want to achieve. Owens, Wallace, and Waldman (2015) used Burns and colleagues' peer ratings on leadership measures to assess an individual's leadership skills and round-robin peer ratings leadership and transitional leadership evaluation. The report on peer evaluation resulted in positive leader emergence and negative leader effectiveness.

Another form of other-report is the NPI-40, which was used by Nevicka et al. (2018), and Chatterjee and Hambrick's prominence of the CEO photograph in the annual report (Braun, 2017). The narcissistic leader evaluation performed by employees, followers, or coworkers is a more credible form of assessment than the leader assessment as it demonstrates the opinions that others have of leaders. It eliminates the bias associated with a narcissistic tendency to enhance and exaggerate one's positive leadership attributes (Judge, LePine, & Rich, 2015). Nevicka et al. (2018) have presented another method of others' evaluation, which uses the followers' self-esteem levels. The authors claimed that followers have a favorable perception of narcissistic leaders when their self-esteem is high; however, the narcissistic leaders are perceived as abusive when the subordinates have low self-esteem (Nevicka et al., 2018). Nevertheless, the research findings stated that others' assessments (employees, followers, and subordinates) are more critical and objective than the narcissistic leaders' self-reports.

Perception of Narcissistic Leaders

Narcissistic individuals have dominant characteristics that are typical of the narcissistic personality. These characteristics influence the opinions that the people surrounding the narcissists have of them. A similar correlation is visible in organizational settings. The perception of a narcissistic leader in organizations is usually one-sided – it is either positive or negative, and there is no middle ground. The research showed that very few people with narcissistic personalities can balance their strong negative features (Nevicka et al., 2013) and less visible positive traits (Owens, Wallace, & Waldman, 2015). Therefore, the subordinates of such leaders almost always see them either positively or negatively. Researchers have argued that both the positive and negative perceptions have various causes, mostly related to the personality traits of such individuals (Baar, 2015; Braun, 2017; Grijalva et al., 2015; Nevicka et al., 2018). Ong et al. (2016) and Korhonen (2017) have also demonstrated that leadership emergence and leadership effectiveness play a crucial role in the narcissistic leader's perception. The current literature has presented other reasons that explain why people have a negative opinion of narcissistic leaders, including cognitive processes (Keller Hansbrough & Jones, 2014), cultural differences (Xiaohong et al., 2018), and the followers' personality traits (Mainah & Perkins, 2016). Therefore, the literature review on this subject was necessary because it presented the negative and positive perceptions of the organization's narcissistic leader. It also identified significant causes that lead to a narcissistic leader being perceived positively or negatively because it influences followers' opinions of narcissistic leaders.

Negative Perception of a Narcissistic Leader

Research has already analyzed the negative impact that the narcissistic leader has on their subordinates. One of the core elements that lead to destructive narcissistic leadership and, therefore, the negative perception of such leaders is the time factor. The longer a narcissistic leader spent with their followers, the more the opinion of the leader worsened. This aspect of the negative perception of a narcissistic leader has been presented by Carlson, Vazire, and Oltmanns (2011). Their study on narcissism noted that new acquaintances perceive the narcissistic individual in a much brighter perspective in opposition to the family members or long-term friends and subordinates, who perceive them negatively. The reason for it was that the family spends more time with the narcissist and is thus familiar with their negative side. The research has also shown that narcissistic individuals wrongly assume that their close friends and family perceive them in a positive light and rate them positively (Carlson, Vazire, & Oltmanns, 2011). Korhonen (2017) added to the conversation stating that when the employees have limited contact with narcissistic leaders and are exposed only to their positive attributes, some organizational citizenship behavior dimensions are elevated. However, when employees are subject to long-term contact with such a leader, it negatively affects their corporate loyalty, civic virtue, sportsmanship, and individual initiative (Korhonen, 2017). Nevicka et al. (2018b) also identified a time factor in their research, stating that the longer the followers or subordinates observed their leaders, the more likely that the relationship became a negative one.

Leadership emergence and leadership effectiveness are other factors that determine whether a narcissistic leader is perceived positively or negatively. They have also been related to the time factor. Ong et al. (2016) noticed that leadership effectiveness is achieved by assessing a leader's performance. Leader emergence is attained through social status in a group (Ong et al., 2016). The authors concluded that people who are more narcissistic have stronger leader emergence tendencies; therefore, it is easier for them to become leaders in a short amount of time after being hired. As Brunell et al. (2008) stated, this correlates with narcissistic fantasies about power, desire for leadership roles, and dominance over others. By observing them for 30 seconds, they found that such leaders possess great confluence in relationship initiation skills and likability (Brunell et al., 2008). Thus, within a few minutes of the first meeting, narcissists charm people with their intelligence and interpersonal skills (Czarna & Nevicka, 2019).

However, researchers have also found that the chances of narcissistic individuals becoming leaders drop dramatically when followers or coworkers get to know them better. This also impacts the leader-employee relationship; thus, leaders lose their attractiveness (Ong et al., 2016). Existing research has shown that such a perception is associated with the negative traits that a narcissistic leader may possess. Narcissistic leaders have an autocratic leadership style that is fueled by their desire to demonstrate their power and micromanage others (Czarna & Nevicka, 2019). Sedikides and Campbell (2017) have added that the narcissists' need for power and dominance may lead to unethical behavior, which negatively affects employees. Hence, narcissistic leaders are inadequate and ineffective.

In their research, Nevicka and her colleagues (2018a) demonstrate that narcissists excel at interviews and attain jobs as leaders with minimum effort due to their personal charm, self-assured body movements, and humorous verbal expressions. However, their research also found that the interview processes did not ensure that narcissistic leaders had organizational experience, which resulted in their poor performance as leaders overall (Nevicka et al., 2018a). It yet has been shown that the leadership emergence leans toward the favorable opinion of the narcissistic leader. In contrast, leadership effectiveness of these leaders is low and contributes to a negative perception of these leaders from their followers.

Cognitive processes visible among people with narcissistic personalities are yet another factor that leads to a negative perception of narcissistic leaders among their subordinates. In their study, Keller Hansbrough and Jones (2014) developed a model that explains that the narcissistic leader's abusive supervision depends on the leader's cognitive processes. Narcissistic leaders perceive these processes as acceptable and typical for the leader's behavior. Braun et al. (2016) called those processes CWB, which are the voluntary actions or processes that hurt an organization and their colleagues. One of the core behaviors that such leaders have are feelings of grandiosity and entitlement and unjustified credit taking. Nevicka et al. (2018a, b) spoke of such a practice of abusive supervision which leads to employees' lower performance at work and even job burnout. The authors also mentioned in their research that when the narcissists' ego is threatened, they tend to become aggressive and derogate others (Nevicka et al., 2018). Keller Hansbrough and Jones (2014) added in their study that narcissistic leaders claim that some of their actions are responses to their employees' insubordination. Nevertheless, such behavior has been perceived by subordinates as abusive and aggressive and brings a negative outcome on the leadership-follower relationship.

The negative perception of narcissistic leaders has also been examined through the prism of workplace bullying and unfairness in the workplace. In their study, Liu et al. (2017) noticed that when higher-level managers mistreated narcissistic leaders, those leaders at times took their anger out on their subordinates. The researchers discovered that the leaders' narcissistic behavior toward their employees negatively impacted the workers' prosocial behavior, such as helping with new hires or staying late to help other coworkers. The low prosocial behavior of workers has also been associated with leader narcissism and self-interested behavior (Liu et al., 2017). This finding indicates that negative narcissistic behavior does not necessarily radiated from the narcissist himself but can also be the side effect of workplace bullying from higher-level managers. Tokarev et al. (2017) also found that each time a subordinate felt that their leader bullied them, they would label the leader as a narcissistic or psychopathic leader.

Further research in this matter has revealed that narcissists bully their subordinates because they act like they are superior to others and have a grandiose self-concept (Tokarev et al., 2017). Narcissistic behavior expressed by leaders harms employees, causes psychological distress, and leads to work-related depression. This explains the negative perception of narcissistic leaders by their followers. Zhi-Hui et al. (2018) and colleagues have noticed a similar correlation between perceptions and narcissistic leaders' workplace bullying toward their subordinates. Their study, in which they researched narcissistic leaders at supervisory levels concerning the LMX, argued that supervisor narcissism leads to employees forming negative perceptions of the leaders, thus silencing employees. To protect their interests, many subordinates remain silent; thus, they fear their leaders. They also withhold any initiative and creativity because it may upset their supervisor (Zhi-Hui et al., 2018).

The perception of narcissistic leaders also depends on the follower's personality. Mainah and Perkins' (2016) research indicated that narcissistic leaders are only seen as abusive by followers with low self-esteem; thus, these followers are more vulnerable to narcissistic leaders. The authors have reported that those with high self-esteem do not perceive the narcissistic leader as abusive (Mainah & Perkins, 2016). However, increased awareness of what narcissism is may reduce follower stress and equip followers with skills to manage and make a narcissistic leader more accountable and ethical; this would then reduce the prevalence of narcissistic leadership and increase organizational success and well-being. Nevicka et al. (2018a) have also found that followers with low self-esteem and low core evaluation were the main subjects of narcissistic leaders' abusive behavior. This is also why these followers perceive narcissistic leaders negatively.

The other elements influencing a narcissistic leader's perception are the form of narcissism and its associated personality traits. A study by Hart et al. (2017) has shown that there are two types of narcissism visible in the office setting: grandiose and vulnerable narcissist self-presentation. The study found that grandiose narcissism is associated with a higher endorsement of self-presentation tactics as a means to make a positive impression. Vulnerable narcissism is associated with more unique qualities of narcissism such as entitlement and insecure feelings of superiority due to the fear of being negatively evaluated by people (Hart et al., 2017). The study showed that different types of narcissism are linked with various profiles of self-presentation. It differed from previous studies because it showed that the opinions of employees or significant others influence narcissistic individuals' perceptions. It also showed that this influence depends on the form of narcissism that a narcissistic person represents. Nevicka et al. (2018b) also found that narcissists tend to be positively perceived by their followers due to their personal charm, self-assured body movements, and humorous verbal expression. Features such as arrogance, overconfidence, or exploitativeness are mostly linked with a negative perception of the narcissistic leader.

The other aspect influencing the perception of a narcissistic leader is people's nationality and culture. Most studies on narcissism have been conducted in individualistic cultures such as the United States, where "Generation Me" is on the rise. However, researchers have also started examining the phenomena of a narcissistic leader in collectivistic cultures such as in China. Xiaohong and his colleagues (2018) researched the role of collectivism (collective culture) on the organization's perception of a narcissistic leader. The authors used the reciprocity method to measure narcissistic leadership on employee knowledge sharing (Xiaohong et al., 2018). The study showed that narcissistic leadership reduces employee information sharing. Furthermore, collectivism has created a boundary in which narcissistic leaders could affect employee knowledge sharing. It means that teamwork or collective work is more important than individual traits such as those of a narcissistic leader (Xiaohong et al., 2018).

Positive Perception of a Narcissistic Leader

Narcissists have not only been perceived as negative people, but they also were valuable assets to the organization. Owens, Wallace, and Waldman (2015) added in their research that narcissists are not one-dimensional individuals but rather a combination of various characteristics that define and influence their level of narcissism. The authors pointed out that if narcissism is associated with other features such as humility, it alleviates the toxic characteristics of narcissistic personalities (Owens, Wallace, & Waldman, 2015). The authors also pointed out that subordinates of narcissistic leaders favored features such as persistence in pursuing goals or risk-taking. Lastly, they found that narcissistic leaders are far more effective, bring value to the company, and are seen in a positive light among their subordinates or followers. Braun (2017) added in her research that a positive perception of a narcissistic leader is linked with narcissistic traits such as charismatic and visionary qualities. These traits are viewed as motivating and inspiring followers. Therefore, subordinates perceive narcissistic leaders favorably due to these traits.

The form of narcissism also contributes to the way that followers view narcissistic leaders. Researchers have noticed that vulnerable narcissism traits have been associated with the narcissist's fear of criticism, which motivates such individuals to try hard to be seen in a positive light by their subordinates (Nevicka et al., 2018b). Vulnerable narcissism has been associated with entitlement, self-absorbance, and the need for attention. However, as opposed to grandiose narcissism, a person with vulnerable narcissism is shy, passive-aggressive, has low self-esteem, and has depression, anxiety, and hypersensitivity, which may be related to being neglected and belittled in the past (Rogoza et al., 2018). Individuals with vulnerable narcissism features are less likely to negatively influence the people they work with or surround themselves with. Therefore, followers see such individuals as positive leaders.

Some of the leader's prototypical traits are also linked with a positive perception of the narcissistic leader. Researchers have found that some of the core features of a narcissist are desirable traits among the leaders or CEOs of large organizations, and these were called the bright side of the narcissistic leader (Nevicka et al., 2018a, b). According to Nevicka et al. (2018a, b), among the preferable characteristics that are sought in leaders are charm, charisma, great vision, and a sense of humor. In Keller Hansbrough and Jones' (2014) theory of a good leader, such a person should help employees during times of uncertainty with their enthusiasm and decisiveness. These traits are admired by employees of organizations. When narcissists showed that they had these features, their followers often had favorable opinions about their supervisor or leader.

The perception of narcissistic leaders is also related to the employees' perception of overall justice represents their global evaluation of fairness in an organization. Ambrose and Schminke (2009) noticed that employees' perceived overall justice positively affected their behavior and outcomes. High organizational justice improves the leader-subordinate relationship and increases employees' positive perception of their bosses, commitment to the organization, and job satisfaction (Ambrose and Schminke, 2009). As a result, employees assess their leaders favorably. In addition, Brunell et al. (2008) stated that subordinates are more likely to accept their leader's behavior performance and evaluate the boss if overall justice in an organization is perceived to be high. When employees feel that they are being treated fairly by their narcissistic leaders, they tend to view them positively and maintain a good relationship with them. Overall, if a narcissistic leader maintains justice in the organization, potential negative consequences brought about by such individuals are reduced, leader-subordinate conflicts are eliminated, and further contribute to an improved LMX (Brunell et al., 2008).

Discussion

The evidence presented has shown that narcissistic leaders can be perceived dually by their followers: either in a positive or negative light. It is also noticeable that various motives guide subordinates to ether opinions. There have been verified multiple causes that lead to a negative perception of a narcissistic leader in the organizations. These are mostly related to the personality traits of narcissistic individuals (Mainah & Perkins, 2016; Nevicka et al., 2018b). The most common negative features of such a person are arrogance, dominance, ruthlessness, greed for power, selfishness, and many others. These features are linked with the grandiose form of narcissism (Hart et al., 2017). Other contributors to the negative perception of narcissistic leaders are the time factor (Carlson, Vazire, & Oltmanns, 2011; Korhonen, 2017; Nevicka et al. 2018b) and the leadership emergence and effectiveness model (Ong et al., 2016). It exemplifies that the more time a follower spends with their leader, the less favorable the opinion they have about the narcissistic leader. The other significant cause of the negative perception of narcissistic leaders is workplace bullying and abusive supervision (Zhi-Hui et al., 2018; Liu et al., 2017; Tokarev et al., 2017).

Despite the negative perception of narcissistic leaders, followers also have favorable opinions of their leaders. Researchers have shown that when a leader displays vulnerable narcissist traits, the leader can be helpful and beneficial to the organization and its employees (Nevicka et al., 2018a, b; Rogoza et al., 2018). Furthermore, leaders' prototypical traits play a crucial role in employees' attitudes toward their leaders; thus, the decisiveness, charisma, and charm of a leader can lead a company to success (Keller Hansbrough & Jones, 2014; Nevicka et al., 2018). The indication for further research is to examine the perception of a narcissistic leader in the organization through the prism of various leader evaluation methods.

Outcomes of a Narcissistic Leader on Employees

A narcissistic leader may seem like a great leader for the organization due to their personality traits. Some of the core features that make such a person a perfect fit for the position are their grand vision, personal charm, and charisma, which allow them to stand out as oppose to other workers and make them likable among employees (Nevicka et al., 2013). Other valuable traits of narcissistic personality that such leaders possess improve the company's overall functioning and increase their financial success; thus, such people take bold risks and are persistent in their pursuit of achieving goals (Owens, Wallace, & Waldman, 2015). Such individuals also lead the organization to innovation and evolution and display authority when in groups (Sedikides & Campbell, 2017). Although the former traits contribute positively to organizational growth and innovation, the second set of characteristics put narcissistic leaders in a much darker perspective, making them look like a tyrant. It is linked with a need for power, abusive supervision, arrogance, and overinflated beliefs in one's capabilities and dominance (Nevicka et al., 2013). The current literature has examined both aspects of the narcissistic personality and has measured the influence of such behavior on the narcissistic leader's employees and followers. The research review shows that nearly 56% of employees in the United States had to deal at least once with a toxic leader (O'Reilly & Chatman, 2020). The number shows that it is a bit over half of working population, which indicates the severity of the phenomena.

Negative Outcome

The research has found that narcissistic leaders can negatively impact their followers, especially when they are dominant and implement abusive supervision (Nevicka et al., 2018). Such supervision takes the form of verbal and other non-physical behaviors rather than physical contact. Nevicka and colleagues (2018) noticed that abusive supervision had very negative consequences on employees because it caused job burnout and lower performance. Over time, this was harmful to the entire organization. Abusive supervision has also been analyzed in relation to the task performance of both leaders and followers. Studies have found that abusive leaders tend to exploit their workers by making them focus on attention to details on the jobs and achieving higher goals (Campbell et al., 2011). Furthermore, narcissistic leaders tend to take credit for others' work, which leads to lower job commitment and tension at the workplace between the leader and subordinates (Keller Hansbrough & Jones 2014). This then can be distilled to the essential aspect of receiving proper gratitude and appreciation for a job well done, even if it is in the form of a simple "thank you." The leaders' need for glory, which results in unethical behavior associated with credit taking and bragging about jobs performed by others, provokes distrust among followers (Hua-Qiang et al., 2018). Employees feel the unjust and lack of regard for their hard work, which then lowers their job satisfaction.

Narcissistic leadership also has a negative influence on employees' interpersonal behavior and their ability to voice their opinions. Liao et al. (2017) reported that depending on the leaders' intention (self-centered or employee-centered intentions) for their impression management, followers might react adversely. When the employees' needs are not met in impression management, they tend to withdraw from work and social interactions with the leader. Impression management is focused on personal interest and the success of a narcissistic leader. The lack of a relationship between the leader and their followers can lower proactivity and engagement at work (Liao et al., 2017). Such an employee may also feel oppressed by their leader and may be afraid of voicing their opinions, thus remaining silent. The silent subordinate then never gives their view and insight into their team's functioning and that of the entire organization, which is harmful to both the employee and the company.

The other essential aspect of employee outcome is psychological safety at work, which can be determined by analyzing stress and depression. Researchers examined that autocratic leadership visible among narcissistic leaders creates distress (Hua-Qiang et al., 2018). When a worker feels suppressed and exploited by a narcissistic leader, their stress levels are elevated because they cannot cope with the tasks and hostile supervision. Keller Hansbrough and Jones (2014) suggested that high stress levels may lead to depression and increase one's intention to quit their job.

The negative impact of a narcissistic leader on employees can also be perceived from the perspective of time. The longer the narcissists is in a leadership position and guides people, the less effective they becomes in their actions, which may even bring the company to bankruptcy and, in the long run, to the loss of many employees (Campbell et al., 2011).

The researchers have also linked the non-productive narcissistic tendencies to the employees' job attitude. Boswell and colleagues (2019) noted in their study that non-productive narcissistic leaders have a terrible influence on employees' attitudes toward work. It results in high turnover among the employees. However, the productive leaders had no impact on the job satisfaction and job attitude of their subordinates. The study presented no indication of the gender aspect; thus, male and female employees are affected differently, but with the same negative result and dissatisfaction with their job. authors also mentioned that a higher level of employees, such as supervisors, middle managers, and executives, are far less tolerant of their leaders' narcissistic behavior (Boswell, Sansberry, & Stout, 2019).

The elevated ego of a narcissistic leader can also be a cause of high employee turnover. Sosik, Chun, and Zhu (2014) mentioned that destructive narcissism is the leading cause of workers' need to quit their job because they feel less happy with their daily tasks and assignments. It is related to their bosses' poor supervision, such as lack of proper information regarding the assigned project or no feedback on already performed work. Often, toxic leaders want the glory for themselves; therefore, they block their subordinates from access on the outcome of the project to get the credit for others' hard work (Sosik, Chun, & Zhu, 2014). O'Reilly and Chatman (2020) add in their study that when leaders' egos get threatened or intimidated, they abuse their power to fire those who challenged them. Such leaders also create a culture that is low in integrity and teamwork. In addition, they also perceive others as the less competent, although they tend to engage in unethical behavior such as stealing, cheating, or lying. The research also showed that in 2018, 73% of employees claimed to work under the supervision of a toxic boss who was aggressive toward them, undermined their work, and blamed them for any work misconduct (O'Reilly & Chatman, 2020). The study also proved that people who worked under the supervision of destructive leaders tend to quit their jobs two years sooner as opposed to those who had a transformational leader (O'Reilly & Chatman, 2020).

The literature review presented that narcissistic leaders had a significant impact on employees' morale at work. Individuals working under the supervision of a toxic boss stated to have less enthusiasm coming to work and felt demotivated to perform their tasks or try-hard. The reason for it was the marginalization of employees over non-merit jobs (Sosik, Chun, & Zhu, 2014). O'Reilly and Chatman (2020) added that the destructive behavior of a narcissistic leader resulted in 38% of work quality among his followers. It means that subordinates who were constantly criticized by their superiors put very little effort into performing well at work due to lack of recognition. Wisse, Barelds, and Rietzschel (2015) adds that more powerful people who express narcissistic personality traits tend to undermine the potential positive effect on innovation of lower hierarchy levels.

Positive Outcome

It has been noticed by the researcher that there is a possible positive connection between narcissistic leaders and their followers, but only when organizations lay out the proper environment for the two sides to work well. As Hannah Helfrich (2018) mentioned, such situations are named "the organic design." These designs aim to create flexible and fast conditions, allowing both sides to work more like partners. It is also advised to implement flat hierarchies and lateral communication, leading to self-organized teams and empowered followers. Researchers have suggested that if leaders abandon the autocratic leadership style and focus on partnerships, the outcomes are more beneficial for their followers and the entire team. Studies have also reported that when that bright side of a narcissist is activated as well as turning an individual into a productive leader, such a person can use their interpersonal skills to turn the entire team and even the organization into a productive one (Campbell et al., 2011). The creative side of narcissistic leaders can also be beneficial to the company. They have excellent capabilities in creating a vision future vision for the company they work for. Unless their vision is not disrupted by narcissist egos and the urge for power, they usually become very successful in achieving that goal.

Narcissistic leaders can also have a significant impact on their followers' careers. This interdependence occurs in organizations with high reward interdependence within the team if the team is rewarded for the group outcome. It results in higher engagement of narcissistic individuals and promotion of his persona to be a team leader. Team members trust the success that a narcissistic leader will bring the team because it will elevate the group in the organizational settings (Nevicka et al., 2011). It has also been said by Wang (2021) that a narcissistic leader who expresses positive traits of this personality can positively impact team followership. Such a leader can positively influence team progress, recognition, and execution ability among the entire organization. Under the leadership of such a boss, the team can grow and achieve success (Wang, 2021). In her study, Wang also examines the impact of "guanxi" on the leader-employee followership. Guanxi in Chinese is known as having personal trust and a strong relationship with someone and can involve moral obligations and exchanging favors. The researcher states that when the supervisor-subordinate guanxi is positive, a leader has more understanding of employee's work-life balance. At the same time, subordinates have more trust and support for their leader (Law et al., 2000).

The relationship between a narcissistic leader and his employees can be seen as positive also when subordinates take on a more submissive role. Wang (2021) has stated in her search that narcissistic leaders are known as the dominant, controlling, and on the constant chase for power. Therefore, they seem to be in ongoing competition with their subordinates, especially the intelligent ones. Such leaders feel threatened and intimidated by the intelligence of their employees and cause tension at work. Wang (2021) mentions that subordinates' submissive approach usually reduces tension and negative impact of narcissistic leaders on employees to some extent; thus, leaders no longer feel intimidated. In addition, the traditionality of some individuals and nations is also helpful in moderating the relationship between narcissistic leaders and their workers by reducing the destructive effect of such leaders on their supervisors and further employees. It results in avoidance of unnecessary competition and conflicts.

Positive outcomes can also be viewed from the perspective of narcissists. Studies have provided evidence that narcissists use their favorable traits to embrace their employees. When workers perform well, they praise their leader, making them look even better as a leader (Campbell et al., 2011). The narcissist feels good about themselves, thus fulfilling their inflated ego and need for glory (Nevicka et al., 2013). Furthermore, since narcissists perceive themselves as superior performers and possess extreme overconfidence and arrogance, they may naturally believe that other team members require their excellence to perform well as a group. If the group performs well, narcissists get the glory for doing an excellent job as team leaders. Such activity enhances narcissistic ego and high self-esteem (Nevicka et al., 2011).

Some studies have examined the impact of narcissistic CEO on employees' change-oriented organizational citizenship behavior (OCB-CH). OCB-CH refers to constructive efforts by individuals to identify and implement changes with respect to work methods, policies, and procedures to improve the situation and performance (Ha et al., 2020). The study performed by Ha et al. (2020) shows that narcissistic leaders' self-confidence, authority, extrovertist, and sociable behavior play important antecedents of employees' OCB-CH. Furthermore, social exchange theorists have suggested that subordinates like their leader's extrovert and sociable character and build reciprocity and mutual trust with the leader; therefore, leader narcissism can positively affect subordinates' OCB-CH. (Ha et al., 2020). In addition, subordinates are likely to believe that narcissistic leaders' extraversion is matched with leadership effectiveness; the employees will view extrovert and narcissistic leaders as more effective. Finally, the positive view of an employer encourages subordinates to conduct innovative behavior that is not officially part of their job in the organization but is beneficial to workers and organizational performance (Campbell et al., 2011).

Some researchers have suggested that narcissistic leaders are beneficial because they create positive outcomes for the organization and followers at the first stage of their leadership career (Campbell et al., 2011). In the emerging zone, when the narcissistic individual is first placed in a problematic organizational situation, such as a chaotic and disorganized one, they are perceived as a positive and valuable persona who can solve the problems. The followers benefit, and the leaders' actions bring order to the previously chaotic organization.

Negative Outcome on Organization

Narcissistic leaders are a threat to their subordinates or coworkers and the company they work for. One of the core damage that a toxic leader does is embedding narcissistic personality traits in his employees. Mickey Butts (2020) compares narcissistic leadership to a colorful saying that the "fish rots from the head down," which means that employees see leaders acting like an ignorant, and they become ignorant, too. Leaders, in general, have a significant impact on their workers' behavior; thus, people look up to them and want to obtain similar behavior which leads to success. Therefore, they not only acquire the good personality features but also the negative ones. It is worth mentioning that not all behavior and actions are worth copying; because it turns people into toxic individuals. In his article, the author has mentioned that it is not entirely about mimicking the boss's behavior but more so about the toxic leader creating a culture at work where people act less ethically (Butts, 2020). Rovelli and Curnis (2020) come to a similar conclusion while conducting a study on 172 Italian CEOs. The authors add that destructive "leaders rise a plague of toadies, opportunists, and enablers guided by self-interests and short on scruples" (Rovelli & Curnis, 2020).

Research also shows that narcissistic leaders play a lot of favoritism at work, by promoting employees who in their favor. O'Reilly and Chatman (2020) noticed that toxic leaders promote people with similar toxic traits to other leadership positions. Such action assures that no other individual will try to rein them on his way to success. People with similar personality traits think and act alike; therefore, they will have the same sense of business and company culture. A narcissistic leader can use those individuals as their allies to create a workplace with obedient employees who work for the glory of their boss. Narcissistic CEOs also hinder the communication flow, which makes it challenging to navigate projects in the organization. Employees receive partial or sometimes no information, leading to chaos and making them less satisfied with their job.

The impact of a toxic leader is this much more destructive to the company because subordinates affected by narcissist's negative behavior carry it in long after the leader is removed from the company. They become less collaborative regardless if they are narcissists or not. The research has also examined how toxic leaders change the organizational culture in the company they work for. O'Reilly and Chatman (2020) present in their study that narcissistic boss changes the corporate culture through the new policies and directories, which fail to bring order to the firm. Instead, those practices create chaos and refrain from governing ethical behavior, assuring equality between man and woman, and fail to prevent conflicts of interest. In addition, narcissistic leaders promote less ethical and collective behavior. Authors notice that a lack of collaboration between coworkers leads to an inability to attain collective accomplishments. Employees are more focused on gaining their individual goals and achievements; therefore, they pay less attention to their company goals (O'Reilly & Chatman, 2020). When subordinates get punished for wrongdoing, their morale sink, their ability to grow and learn weakens; therefore, they have fewer opportunities to gain new experience. All in all, the entire company as an organization suffers due to unethical and non-collaborative work culture.

Along with the change made to the organization's culture, toxic leaders also introduce and engage in illegal actions, sometimes leading to white-collar crime. Researchers warn that narcissistic leaders are like a slow poison to the company (Rovelli & Curnis, 2020). Narcissistic individuals present a great first impression during their interview process, and in the first few months of working in the company, they get promoted quicker. Braun (2017) mentions that the fast advancement of destructive leaders puts the business at risk with younger inexperienced individuals, who are more willing to engage in illegal behavior. The author presented that narcissistic leaders who are unethical and overconfident of being always right more often undergo regulatory investigations of ethical breaches (Braun, 2017). Such individuals also generate lower financial performance, engage in financial crime and tax avoidance. O'Reilly and Chatman (2020) add that many external and competitive variables can affect stock prices, revenues, and profitability. Narcissistic CEOs are often overconfident with their ability to achieve big earnings; therefore, they tend to use financial manipulations to reach their assigned goal. In addition, the research shows that toxic leaders involve chief financial officers in financial misreporting, which puts companies at risk (O'Reilly & Chatman, 2020). Recently, global companies such as WeWork or Uber engaged in severe lapses in ethical conduct. Narcissistic leaders believe they are extraordinarily talented and endowed with superior qualities such as intelligence, competence, innovativeness, and leadership, which give them the right to think highly of their ability to perform as CEOs (O'Reilly & Chatman, 2020).

The actions of narcissistic leaders also affect a firm's internal hierarchy. Wisse, Barelds, and Rietzschel (2015) noticed that toxic bosses undermine the positive effect on innovativeness in the lower levels of a firm's hierarchy. Often destructive leaders put less attention to promoting people from lower levels, especially those whose work may undermine or overshine his work. Lack of ability for advancement at work brings chaos and disorientation among employees, causing lower motivation and job performance.

The other negative outcome of the leadership of a narcissistic leader is over-investment and possible revenue loss. Narcissists are known to be visionaries and risk-taking individuals. Such individuals are overconfident of their ability to deliver the work they promise are not afraid to propose risky investments. O'Reilly and Chatman (2020) state that grandiose narcissistic CEOs engage in more acquisitions and are likely to overpay for them. Although it seems like a fantastic move for the company because the firm can be up to date with new technology and innovation; however, such action, in the end, may create very little value to the company. The study has shown that risky investments may result in quick money returns when the market is on the rise and cause substantial financial losses when the market turns down.

References

Ackerman, R., Witt, E., Brent Donnellan, M., Trzesniewski, K., Robins, R., & Kashy, D. (2011). What does the narcissistic personality inventory really measure? *Assessment* 18: 67–87. https://www.ncbi.nlm.nih.gov/pubmed/20876550

Adams, J. (2015). The relationship of managers' power motivations to personality pathology. https://scholarworks.waldenu.edu/dissertations/1333/

Ambrose, M. L., & Schminke, M. (2009). The role of overall justice judgments in organizational justice research: A test of mediation. *Journal of Applied Psychology* 94: 491–500.

American Psychiatric Association. (2013). *Diagnostic and Statistical Manual of Mental Disorders* (*DSM-5*®), Fifth Edition. https://www.appi.org/Diagnostic_and_Statistical_Manual_of_Mental_Disorders_DSM-5_Fifth_Edition

Ames, R., Rose, P., & Anderson, C. (2006). The NPI-16 as a short measure of narcissism. *Journal of Research in Personality* 40: 440–450. https://www.sciencedirect.com/science/article/abs/pii/S0092656605000504, https://www.researchgate.net/publication/346797502_Impact_of_narcissistic_leadership_on_employee_work_outcomes_in_banking_sector_of_Pakistan

Asrar-ul-Haq, M., & Anjum, T. (2020). Impact of narcissistic leadership on employee work outcomes in banking sector of Pakistan. *Future Business Journal* 6: 34.

Baars, S. (2015). Narcissistic leadership. https://docplayer.net/56209673-Narcissistic-leadership.html

Babiak, P., & Hare, R. D. (2006). *Snakes in Suits: When Psychopaths Go to Work*. Regan Books/Harper Collins Publishers.

Besser, A., & Priel, B. (2010). Grandiose narcissism versus vulnerable narcissism in threatening situations: Emotional reactions to achievement failure and interpersonal rejection. *Journal of Social and Clinical Psychology* 29(8): 874–902. https://www.researchgate.net/publication/282637006_Grandiose_Narcissism_Versus_Vulnerable_Narcissism_in_Threatening_Situations_Emotional_Reactions_to_Achievement_Failure_and_Interpersonal_Rejection

Bhasin, H. (2019, October 18). Abuse of power at workplace – meaning, examples and impacts. Marketing91. https://www.marketing91.com/abuse-of-power-at-workplace/

Bierhoff, H., Margraf, J., & Brailovskaia, J. (2019). How to identify narcissism with 13 items? Validation of the German Narcissistic Personality Inventory–13 (G-NPI-13). *Assessment* 26: 630–644. https://journals.sagepub.com/doi/full/10.1177/1073191117740625

Bilotta, E., Carcione, A., Fera, T., Moroni, F., Nicolò, G., Pedone, R., . . . Colle, L. (2018). Symptom severity and mindreading in narcissistic personality disorder. *PLoS ONE* 13(8): e0201216. https://doi.org/10.1371/journal.pone.0201216

Blair, C., Hoffman, B., & Helland, K. (2008). Narcissism in organizations: A multisource appraisal reflects different perspectives. *Human Performance* 21: 254–276. https://link.springer.com/chapter/10.1007/978-3-319-60330-8_4

Blonigen, D. M., Patrick, C. J., Douglas, K. S., Poythress, N. G., Skeem, J. L., Lilienfeld, S. O., . . . Krueger, R. F. (2010). Multi-method assessment of psychopathy in relation to factors of internalizing and externalizing from the Personality Assessment Inventory: The impact of method variance and suppressor effects. *Psychological Assessment* 22: 96–107. http://dx.doi.org/10.1037/a0017240

Boddy, C. R. (2014). Corporate psychopaths, conflict, employee affective well-being and counterproductive work behaviour. *Journal of Business Ethics* 121: 107–121. http://dx.doi.org/10.1007/s10551-013-1688-0

Boswell, S., Sansberry, K. D., & Stout, S. (2019). Narcissistic leaders and their effect on employee work attitudes. *SSRN Electronic Journal*. https://doi.org/10.2139/ssrn.3454128

Brailovskaia, J., Rohmann, E., Bierhoff, H.-W., & Margraf, J. (2020). The anxious addictive narcissist: The relationship between grandiose and vulnerable narcissism, anxiety symptoms and Facebook addiction. *PLoS ONE* 15(11): e0241632. https://doi.org/10.1371/journal.pone.0241632

Braun, S. (2017). Leader narcissism and outcomes in organizations: A review at multiple levels of analysis and implications for future research. *Frontiers in Psychology* 8: 773. https://www.frontiersin.org/articles/10.3389/fpsyg.2017.00773/full

Braun, S., Aydin, N., Frey, D., & Peus, C. (2016). Leader narcissism predicts malicious envy and supervisor-targeted counterproductive work behavior – evidence from field and experimental research. *Journal of Business Ethics* 151: 725–741. http://dro.dur.ac.uk/18920/

Brunell, A., Gentry, W., Campbell, W., Hoffman, B., Kuhnert, K., & Demarree, K. (2008). Leader emergence: The case of the narcissistic leader. *Personality and Social Psychology Bulletin* 34: 1663–1676. https://www.ncbi.nlm.nih.gov/pubmed/18794326

Butts, M. (2020). How narcissistic leaders make organizations less ethical, greater good magazine. https://greatergood.berkeley.edu/article/item/how_narcissistic_leaders_make_organizations_less_ethical

Campbell, K. W., Hoffman, B. J., Campbell, S. M., & Marchisio, G. (2011). Narcissism in organizational contexts. *Human Resource Management Review* 21: 268–284. https://digitalcommons.kennesaw.edu/facpubs/1582/

Camm, T. W. (2014). The dark side of leadership: Dealing with a narcissistic boss mining engineering. https://digitalcommons.mtech.edu/mine_engr/2

Carlson, E., Vazire, S., & Oltmanns, T. (2011). You probably think this paper's about you: Narcissists' perceptions of their personality and reputation. *Journal of Personality and Social Psychology* 101: 185–201. https://www.ncbi.nlm.nih.gov/pmc/articles/PMC3119754/

Carter, G., & Douglass, D. (2018). The aging narcissus: Just a myth? Narcissism moderates the age-loneliness relationship in older age. *Frontiers in Psychology* 9: 1254. https://www.frontiersin.org/articles/10.3389/fpsyg.2018.01254/full

Chatterjee, A., & Hambrick, D. (2007). It's all about me: Narcissistic chief executive officers and their effects on company strategy and performance. *Administrative Science Quarterly* 52: 351–386. https://journals.sagepub.com/doi/abs/10.2189/asqu.52.3.351

Christie, R., & Geis, F. L. (1970). Studies in Machiavellianism. New York: Academic Press.

Clough, P. J., Earle, K., & Sewell, D. (2002). Mental toughness: The concept and its measurement. In: Cockerill I. (ed) *Solutions in Sport Psychology* (pp. 32–43). London: Thomson.

Conger, J. A., & Kanungo, R. N. (2016). The empowerment process: Integrating theory and practice. *The Academy of Management Review* 13(3): 471–482.

Czarna, A., Dufner, M., & Clifton, A. (2014). The effects of vulnerable and grandiose narcissism on liking-based and disliking-based centrality in social networks. *Journal of Research in Personality* 50: 42–45. https://www.sciencedirect.com/science/article/pii/S009265661400018X

Czarna, A., & Nevicka, B. (2019). Narcissism and leadership. In: Zeigler-Hill V., Shackelford T. (eds) *Encyclopedia of Personality and Individual Differences* (pp. 1–9). Springer, Cham. https://link.springer.com/referenceworkentry/10.1007%2F978-3-319-28099-8_2334-1Dawood, S., & Pincus, A. L. (2017). Pathological narcissism and the severity, variability, and instability of depressive symptoms, personality disorders: Theory, research, and treatment. *American Psychological Association* 9(2): 144–154. http://dx.doi.org/10.1037/per0000239

Day, N. J. S., Townsend, M. L., & Grenyer, B. F. S. (2020). Living with pathological narcissism: A qualitative study. *Borderline Personality Disorder and Emotion Dysregulation* 7. https://doi.org/10.1186/s40479-020-00132-8

De Hoogh, A. H. B., Den Hartog, D. N., & Belschak, F. D. (2021). Showing one's true colors: Leader Machiavellianism, rules and instrumental climate, and abusive supervision. *Journal of Organizational Behavior* 42(7): 851–866. https://doi.org/10.1002/job.2536

De Hoogh, A., Hartog, D., & Nevicka, B. (2015). Gender differences in the perceived effectiveness of narcissistic leaders. *Applied Psychology* 64: 473–498. https://onlinelibrary.wiley.com/doi/abs/10.1111/apps.12015

den Hartog, D. N., & Belschak, F. D. (2012). Work engagement and Machiavellianism in the ethical leadership process. *Journal of Business Ethics* 107: 35–47.

Drayton, L. A., Santos, L. R., & Baskin-Sommers, A. (2018). Psychopaths fail to automatically take the perspective of others. *Psychological and Cognitive Sciences* 115: 3302–3307. https://www.pnas.org/content/115/13/3302

Ellwood, B. (2021). Narcissists make their way to CEO positions faster than their counterparts, study finds. PsyPost. https://www.psypost.org/2021/02/narcissists-make-their-way-to-ceo-positions-faster-than-their-counterparts-study-finds-59517

Fatfouta, R. (2019). Facets of narcissism and leadership: A tale of Dr. Jekyll and Mr. Hyde? *Human Resource Management Review*. https://www.sciencedirect.com/science/article/pii/S1053482218302213

Fennimore, A. (2020). That's my stapler: Vulnerable narcissists and organizational territoriality. *Management Research Review*. https://www.researchgate.net/publication/338565575_That's_my_stapler_vulnerable_narcissists_and_organizational_territoriality

Foster, D., Campbell, K., & Twenge, J. (2003). Individual differences in narcissism: Inflated self-views across the lifespan and around the world. *Journal of Research in Personality* 37: 469–486. https://www.sciencedirect.com/science/article/pii/S0092656603000266

Foti, R., Bray, B., Thompson, N., & Allgood, S. (2012). Know thy self, know thy leader: Contributions of a pattern-oriented approach to examining leader perceptions. *The Leadership Quarterly* 23(4): 702–717. https://www.sciencedirect.com/science/article/pii/S1048984312000240

Furtner, M. R., Maran, T., & Rauthmann, J. F. (2017). Dark leadership: The role of leaders' dark triad personality traits. In: Clark M. & Gruber C. W. (eds) *Leader Development Deconstructed* (pp. 75–99). Springer, Cham

Galvin, B., Lange, D., & Ashforth, B. (2014). Narcissistic organizational identification: Seeing oneself as central to the organization's identity. *Academy of Management Review* 40. https://journals.aom.org/doi/abs/10.5465/amr.2013.0103

Galvin, B. M., Waldman, D., & Balthazard, P. A. (2010). Visionary communication qualities as mediators of the relationship between narcissism and attributions of leader charisma. *Personnel Psychology* 63(3): 509–537. https://doi.org/10.1111/j.1744-6570.2010.01179.x

Germain, M. (2017). *Narcissism at Work – Personality Disorders of Corporate Leaders*. New York: Palgrave Macmillan. https://www.palgrave.com/gp/book/9783319603292

George, F. R., & Short, D. (2018). The cognitive neuroscience of narcissism. *Journal of Brain, Behaviour and Cognitive Sciences* 1: 6

Giacomin, M. (2016). Investigating grandiose narcissism as a personality process. https://scholars.wlu.ca/etd/1864/

Goldner-Vukov, M., & Moore, L. J. (2010). Malignant narcissism: From fairy tales to harsh reality. *Psychiatria Danubina* 22(3): 392–405.

Goman, C. K. (2016, March 31). Is your communication style dictated by your gender? *The Little Black Book of Billionaire Secrets* (Forbes). https://www.forbes.com/sites/carolkinseygoman/2016/03/31/is-your-communication-style-dictated-by-your-gender/?sh=68aa4110eb9d

Grenyer, B. F. S. (2013). Historical overview of pathological narcissism. In: Ogrodniczuk J. S. (ed) *Understanding and Treating Pathological Narcissism* (pp. 15–26). American Psychological Associationhttps://www.researchgate.net/publication/259187048_Historical_overview_of_pathological_narcissism

Grijalva, E., Harms, P., Newman, D., Gaddis, B., & Fraley, R. (2015). Narcissism and leadership: A meta-analytic review of linear and nonlinear relationships. *Personnel Psychology* 68: 1–47. https://onlinelibrary.wiley.com/doi/abs/10.1111/peps.12072

Grijalva, E., Newman, D. A., Tay, L., Donnellan, M. B., Harms, P. D., Robins, W., & Tajyi, Y. (2013). Gender differences in narcissism: A meta-analytic review. *Psychological Bulletin* 144(2): 120.

Ha, S-B., Lee, S., Byun, G., & Dai, Y. (2020). Leader narcissism and subordinate change-oriented organizational citizenship behavior: Overall justice as a moderator. *Social Behavioral and Personality* 48(7): e9330. https://doi-org.unh-proxy01.newhaven.edu/10.2224/sbp.9330

Harms, P. (2017). Hogan development survey. https://www.semanticscholar.org/author/Peter-D.-Harms/2332255

Harms, P. D., Spain, S. M., & Hannah, S. T. (2011). Leader development and the dark side of personality. *The Leadership Quarterly* 22: 495–509. http://dx.doi.org/10.1016/j.leaqua.2011.04.007

Harrison, H., Birks, M., Franklin, R., & Mills, J. (2017). Case study research: Foundations and methodological orientations. *Forum: Qualitative Social Research* 18(1). http://www.qualitative-research.net/index.php/fqs/article/view/2655/4079

Hart, W., Adams, J., Burton, A., & Tortoriello, G. (2017). Narcissism and self-presentation: Profiling grandiose and vulnerable narcissists' self-presentation tactic use. *Personality and Individual Differences* 104: 48–57. https://www.sciencedirect.com/science/article/abs/pii/S0191886916308121. https://link.springer.com/article/10.1007/s10551-012-1296-4

Helfrich, H. (2018, May 30). The effect of leader and follower personality on work processes: Analyzing the influence of humility and narcissism. https://core.ac.uk/display/159671212

Hoffman, B., Helland, K., & Blair, C. (2008). Narcissism in organizations: A multisource appraisal reflects different perspectives. *Human Performance* 21(3): 254–276. https://www.tandfonline.com/doi/abs/10.1080/08959280802137705

Hogan, R., & Hogan, J. (2009). *Hogan Development Survey Manual*. Tulsa, OK: Hogan Assessment Systems.

Hua-Qiang, W., Guang-Lei, Z., Zhi-Hui, D., & Zhi-Hui, C. (2018). How supervisor narcissism contributes to employee silence: Roles of negative anticipations and leader–member exchange. *Social Behavior and Personality* 46(4): 653–666. https://www.sbp-journal.com/index.php/sbp/article/view/6815

Hurley, S. (2005). Social heuristics that make us smarter. *Philosophical Psychology* 18: 585–612. https://doi.org/10.1080/09515080500264214

Jauk, E., Weigle, E., Lehmann, K., Benedek, M., & Neubauer, A. (2017). The relationship between grandiose and vulnerable (hypersensitive) narcissism. *Frontiers in Psychology* 8: 1600. https://www.frontiersin.org/articles/10.3389/fpsyg.2017.01600/full

Jones, D., & Paulhus, D. (2014). Introducing the Short Dark Triad (SD3): A brief measure of dark personality traits. *Assessment* 21: 28–41. https://journals.sagepub.com/doi/10.1177/1073191113514105

Judge, T., LePine, J., & Rich, B. (2015). Loving yourself abundantly: Relationship of the narcissistic personality to self- and other perceptions of workplace deviance, leadership, and task and contextual performance. *Journal of Applied Psychology* 91(4): 762–776. https://asu.pure.elsevier.com/en/publications/loving-yourself-abundantly-relationship-of-the-narcissistic-perso

Kacel, E., Ennis, N., & Pereira, D. (2017). Narcissistic personality disorder in clinical health psychology practice: Case studies of comorbid psychological distress and life-limiting illness. *Behavioral Medicine* 43: 156–164. https://chp.phhp.ufl.edu/people/graduate-students/elizabeth-kacel

Kaufman, S. B., Weiss, B., Miller, J. D., & Campbell, W. K. (2020). Clinical correlates of vulnerable and grandiose narcissism: A personality perspective. *Journal of Personality Disorder* 34: 107–130. https://scottbarrykaufman.com/wp-content/uploads/2018/09/Kaufman-Weiss-Miller-Campbell-2018-Clinical-Correlates-of-Vulnerable-and-Grandiose-Narcissism-A-Personality-Perspective.pdf

Keller Hansbrough, T., & Jones, G. (2014). Inside the minds of narcissists: How narcissistic leaders' cognitive processes contribute to abusive supervision.

Zeitschrift für Psychologie 222(4): 214–220. https://econtent.hogrefe.com/doi/10.1027/2151-2604/a000188

Kessler, R. C., McLaughlin, K. A., Green, J. G., Gruber, M. J., Sampson, N.A., Zaslavsky, A. M., . . . Williams DR. (2010). Childhood adversities and adult psychopathology in the WHO World Mental Health Surveys. *British Journal of Psychiatry* 197(5):378–385. doi: 10.1192/bjp.bp.110.080499

Kiazad, K., Restubog, S. L. D., Zagenczyk, T. J., Kiewitz, C., & Tang, R. L. (2010). In pursuit of power: The role of authoritarian leadership in the relationship between supervisors' Machiavellianism and subordinates' perception of abuse supervisory behavior. *Journal of Research in Personality* 44: 512–519. https://www.academia.edu/15862199/In_pursuit_of_power_The_role_of_authoritarian_leadership_in_the_relationship_between_supervisors_Machiavellianism_and_subordinates_perceptions_of_abusive_supervisory_behavior

Kiliç, N., & Eryilmaz, A. (2019). Investigating narcissistic personality traits in the context of positive psychotherapy. *Noro Psikiyatr Ars* 56(1):40–46. doi: 10.29399/npa.22794.

Kohut, H. (1971). *The Analysis of the Self.* New York: International Universities Press. https://www.scirp.org/(S(i43dyn45teexjx455qlt3d2q))/reference/ReferencesPapers.aspx?ReferenceID=1464977

Korhonen, J. (2017, January 01). Effects of narcissistic leadership on organizational citizenship behaviors: A case study on the perceptions of media production company employees. http://jultika.oulu.fi/Record/nbnfioulu-201705252103

Krizan, Z., & Herlache, A. (2017). The narcissism spectrum model: A synthetic view of narcissistic personality. *Personality and Social Psychology Review* 22: 3–31. https://journals.sagepub.com/doi/10.1177/1088868316685018

Kubarych, T. S., Deary, I. J., & Austin, E. J. (2003). The Narcissistic Personality Inventory: Factor structure in a non-clinical sample. *Personality and Individual Differences* 36: 857–872. https://www.sciencedirect.com/science/article/pii/S0191886903001582

Landay, K., Harms, P. D., & Credé, M. (2019). Shall we serve the dark lords? A meta-analytic review of psychopathy and leadership. *Journal of Applied Psychology* 104(1): 183–196. https://www.apa.org/pubs/journals/features/apl-apl0000357.pdf

Lane, J. M., & Kent, S. A., (2008). Malignant narcissism, L. Ron Hubbard, and scientology's policies of narcissistic rage. https://ccgt.nl/pics_act/malignant-narcisme.pdf

Law, K. S., Wong, C. S., Wang, D., & Wang, L. (2000). Effect of supervisor–subordinate guanxi on supervisory decisions in China: An empirical investigation. *International Journal of Human Resource Management* 11: 751–765. https://doi.org/10.1080/09585190050075105

Liao, S., Zhou, X., Guo, Z., & Li, Z. (2017). How does leader narcissism influence employee voice: The attribution of leader impression management and leader-member exchange. *International Journal of Environmental Research and Public Health* 16: 1819. https://www.mdpi.com/1660-4601/16/10/1819

Lilienfeld, S. O., Waldman, I. D., Landfield, K., Watts, A. L., Rubenzer, S., & Faschingbauer, T. R. (2012). Fearless dominance and the U.S. presidency: Implications of psychopathic personality traits for successful and unsuccessful political leadership. *Journal of Personality and Social Psychology* 103: 489–505. http://dx.doi.org/10.1037/a0029392

Liu, H., Chiang, J., Fehr, R., Xu, M., & Wang, S. (2017). How do leaders react when treated unfairly? Leader narcissism and self-interested behavior in response to unfair treatment. *Journal of Applied Psychology* 102(11): 1590–1599. https://insights.ovid.com/applied-psychology/japsy/2017/11/000/leaders-react-when-treated-unfairly-leader/6/00004565

Luo, Y. L. L., & Cia, H. (2018). The etiology of narcissism: A review of behavioral genetic studies. In: Herman A., Brunell A., Foster J. (eds) *Handbook of Trait Narcissism*. Springer, Cham. https://www.springer.com/gp/book/9783319921709

Maccoby, M. (2014, August 01). Narcissistic leaders: The incredible pros, the inevitable cons. https://hbr.org/2004/01/narcissistic-leaders-the-incredible-pros-the-inevitable-cons

Maciantowicz, O., & Zajenkowski, M. (2020). Is narcissistic anger fueled by neuroticism? The relationship between grandiose and vulnerable narcissism, neuroticism, and trait anger. *Current Psychology* 39: 1674–1681. http://icelab.psych.uw.edu.pl/wp-content/uploads/2018/05/maciantowicz-zajenkowski.pdfMainah, F., & Perkins, V. (2016). Narcissism in organizational leadership. http://www.docdatabase.net/more-narcissism-in-organizational-leadership-fredah-mainah--1327285.html

Mathieu, C., & Babiak, P. (2016). Corporate psychopathy and abusive supervision: Their influence on employees' job satisfaction and turnover intentions. *Personality and Individual Differences* 91: 102–106. http://dx.doi.org/10.1016/j.paid.2015.12.002

Megargee, E. (2009, July 14). The California Psychological Inventory. https://oxfordindex.oup.com/view/10.1093/oxfordhb/9780195366877.013.0017

Miller, J., Price, J., Gentile, B., Lynam, D., & Campbell, W. (2012). Grandiose and vulnerable narcissism from the perspective of the interpersonal circumplex. *Personality and Individual Differences* 53: 507–512. https://www.sciencedirect.com/science/article/pii/S0191886912001912

Molm, L. (2010). The structure of reciprocity. *Social Psychology Quarterly* 73: 119–131.

Morey, L., & Stagner, B. (2012). Narcissistic pathology as core personality dysfunction: Comparing the DSM-IV and the DSM-5 proposal for narcissistic personality disorder. *Journal of Clinical Psychology* 68: 908–921. https://onlinelibrary.wiley.com/doi/abs/10.1002/jclp.21895

Muller, R. (2014). What kind of narcissist are you? https://www.academia.edu/7129181/What_Kind_of_Narcissist_Are_You

Nevicka, B., De Hoogh, A., Den Hartog, D., & Belschak, F. (2018a). Narcissistic leaders and their victims: Followers low on self-esteem and low on core self-evaluations suffer most. *Frontiers in Psychology* 9: 422. https://www.frontiersin.org/articles/10.3389/fpsyg.2018.00422/full

Nevicka, B., De Hoogh, A. H., Van Vianen, A. E., & Ten Velden, F. S. (2013). Uncertainty enhances the preference for narcissistic leaders. *European Journal of Social Psychology* 43: 370–380. https://www.narcis.nl/publication/RecordID/oai%3Adare.uva.nl%3Apublications%2F84d8e93b-f2a0-41f4-9475-20a793aeb194

Nevicka, B., Van Vianen, A., De Hoogh, A., & Voorn, B. (2018b). Narcissistic leaders: An asset or a liability? Leader visibility, follower responses, and group-level absenteeism. *Journal of Applied Psychology* 103: 703–723. https://dare.uva.nl/personal/search?identifier=3206d78e-0bdd-43d2-9ba5-98c5d2cd6157

Nevicka, B., Velden, F., Hoogh, A., & Vianen, A. (2011). Reality at odds with perceptions: Narcissistic leaders and group performance. *Psychological Science* 22: 1259–1264. https://journals.sagepub.com/doi/10.1177/0956797611417259

O'Brien, L. T., Major, B. N., & Gilbert, P. N. (2012). Gender differences in entitlement: The role of system-justifying beliefs. *Basic and Applied Social Psychology* 34(2): 136–145. http://dx.doi.org/10.1080/01973533.2012.655630

Olsen, K., Dworkis, K. K., & Young, S. M. (2014). CEO narcissism and accounting: A picture of profits. *Journal of Management Accounting Research* 26(2): 243–267. https://papers.ssrn.com/sol3/papers.cfm?abstract_id=2115067

Ong, C., Roberts, R., Calum, A., Woodman, T., & Akehurst, S. (2016). The leadership is sinking: A temporal investigation of narcissistic leadership. *Journal of Personality* 84: 237–247. https://onlinelibrary.wiley.com/doi/abs/10.1111/jopy.12155

O'Reilly, C., & Chatman, J. A. (2020). Transformational leader or narcissist? How grandiose narcissists can create and destroy organizations and institutions. *California Management Review* 62: 5–27. https://cmr.berkeley.edu/assets/documents/promo/62-3-oreilly.pdf

O'Reilly, C., Doerr, B., Caldwell, D., & Chatman, J. (2014). Narcissistic CEOs and executive compensation. *The Leadership Quarterly* 25: 218–231. https://www.sciencedirect.com/science/article/pii/S1048984313000805

Owens, B., Wallace, A., & Waldman, D. (2015). Leader narcissism and follower outcomes: The counterbalancing effect of leader humility. *Journal of Applied Psychology* 100: 1203–1213. https://asu.pure.elsevier.com/en/publications/leader-narcissism-and-follower-outcomes-the-counterbalancing-effe

Padilla, A., Hogan, R., & Kaiser, R. B. (2007). The toxic triangle: Destructive leaders, susceptible followers, and conducive environments. *The Leadership Quarterly* 18(3): 176–194.

Paulhus, D. L., & Williams, K. M. (2002). The Dark Triad of personality: Narcissism, Machiavellianism, and psychopathy. *Journal of Research in Personality* 36(6): 556–563. https://academic.microsoft.com/paper/1982777740/citedby/search?q=The%20Dark%20Triad%20of%20personality%3A%20Narcissism%2C%20Machiavellianism%2C%20and%20psychopathy&qe=RId%253D1982777740&f=&orderBy=0

Peltokangas, H. (2016). Self-esteem, tenure, and narcissistic leader's performance. Vaasana yliopisto, University of Vaasa. https://www.uwasa.fi/materiaali/pdf/isbn_978-952-476-683-8.pdf

Perez, R. (2017, September 06). Individual executive characteristics and firm performance: Evidence from CEO narcissism. https://scholarsbank.uoregon.edu/xmlui/handle/1794/22658

Pincus, A. L., & Lukowitsky, M. R. (2010). Pathological narcissism and narcissistic personality disorder. *The Annual Review of Clinical Psychology.* 6: 421–426. https://pubmed.ncbi.nlm.nih.gov/20001728/

Raskin, R., & Terry, H. (1988). A principal-components analysis of the Narcissistic Personality Inventory and further evidence of its construct validity. *Journal of Personality and Social Psychology* 54: 890–902. http://dx.doi.org/10.1037/0022-3514.54.5.890

Roberts, B. W., & Robins, R. W. (2000). Broad dispositions, broad aspirations: the intersection of the Big Five dimensions and major life goals. *Personality and Social Psychology Bulletin* 26: 1284–1296. 10.1177/0146167200262009

Rogoza, R., Żemojtel-Piotrowska, M., Kwiatkowska, M., & Kwiatkowska, K. (2018). The bright, the dark, and the blue face of narcissism: The spectrum of narcissism in its relations to the metatraits of personality, self-esteem, and the nomological network of shyness, loneliness, and empathy. *Frontiers in Psychology* 9: 343. https://www.frontiersin.org/articles/10.3389/fpsyg.2018.00343/full

Ronningstam, E., & Baskin-Sommers, A. R. (2013). Fear and decision-making in narcissistic personality disorder – a link between psychoanalysis and neuroscience. *Dialogues in Clinical Neuroscience* 15(2): 191–201. https://www.ncbi.nlm.nih.gov/pmc/articles/PMC3811090/

Rosenthal, S., & Pittinsky, T. (2006). Narcissistic leadership. *The Leadership Quarterly* 17: 617–633. https://www.researchgate.net/profile/Seth_Rosenthal/publication/223046510_Narcissistic_Leadership/links/5d1f5ac192851cf44068903f/Narcissistic-Leadership.pdf

Rosenthal, S. A. (2010). Narcissism and leadership: A review and research agenda. https://dspace.mit.edu/handle/1721.1/55948

Rovelli, P., & Curnis, C. (2020). The perks of narcissism: Behaving like a star speeds up career advancement to the CEO position. https://www.psypost.org/2021/02/narcissists-make-their-way-to-ceo-positions-faster-than-their-counterparts-study-finds-59517

Schyns, J., & Schilling, B. (2012). How bad are the effects of bad leaders? A meta-analysis of destructive leadership and its outcomes. *The Leadership Quarterly* 24: 138–158. https://www.sciencedirect.com/science/article/pii/S1048984312000872

Sedikides, C., & Campbell, K. (2017). Narcissistic force meets systemic resistance: The Energy Clash Model. *Perspectives on Psychological Science* 12: 400–421. https://eprints.soton.ac.uk/404441/1/__filestore.soton.ac.uk_users_gg_mydocuments_constantine%2520publications%2520pdf%2527s_In%2520Press_Sedikides%2520%2520Campbell_in%2520press%2520Perspectives%2520on%2520Psychological%2520Science.pdf

Sedikides, C., Rudich, E. A., Gregg, A. P., Kumashiro, M., & Rusbult, C. (2004). Are normal narcissists psychologically healthy?: Self-esteem matters. *Journal of Personality and Social Psychology* 87: 400–416. https://doi.org/10.1037/0022-3514.87.3.400. https://pubmed.ncbi.nlm.nih.gov/15382988/

Serenko, A., & Choo, C. W. (2020). Knowledge sabotage as an extreme form of counterproductive knowledge behavior: The role of narcissism, Machiavellianism, psychopathy, and competitiveness. *Journal of Knowledge Management* 24(9): 2299–2325. http://aserenko.com/papers/Knowledge_Sabotage_Study_3_Serenko_Choo.pdf

Szabó, E., & Jones, D. N. (2019). Gender differences moderate Machiavellianism and impulsivity: Implications for Dark Triad research. *Personality and Individual Differences* 141: 160–165.

Shurden, S. (2018). A study of the relationship of narcissistic leadership in the accounting profession on job satisfaction: An application of structural equation modeling. *Journal of Finance and Accountancy* 23: 1–19. https://aabri.com/jfa.htmlSimpson, J. (2012, January 01). Self-perception and performance: Exploratory research into the narcissists' first 20 months within a corporate graduate recruitment programme: A dissertation presented in partial fulfilment of the requirements for the degree of Doctor of Philosophy in Human Development Studies at Massey University, Palmerston North, New Zealand. https://mro.massey.ac.nz/handle/10179/4185

Singh, N., Sengupta, S., & Dev, S. (2018, November 5). Toxic leadership: The most menacing form of leadership. https://www.intechopen.com/chapters/60316

Sosik, J. J., Chun, J. U., & Zhu, W. (2014). Hang on to your ego: The moderating role of leader narcissism on relationships between leader charisma and follower psychological empowerment and moral identity. *Journal of Business Ethics* 120: 65–80. https://doi.org/10.1007/s10551-013-1651-0

Stewart, C. (2008, July 25). The validity of the California Psychological Inventory in the prediction of police officer applicant's suitability for employment. https://commons.pacificu.edu/spp/156/

Stinson, F. S., Dawson, D. A., Goldstein, R. B., Chou, P. S., Huang, B., Smith, S. M., . . . Grant, B. F. (2008). Prevalence, correlates, disability, and comorbidity of DSM-IV narcissistic personality disorder: Results from the Wave 2 National Epidemiologic Survey on Alcohol and Related Conditions. *The Journal of Clinical Psychiatry* 69: 1033–1045. https://www.ncbi.nlm.nih.gov/pmc/articles/PMC2669224

Strachey, J. (ed) (2015). *The Standard Edition of the Complete Psychological Works of Sigmund Freud* (Vol. 1–24). https://www.amazon.com/Complete-Psychological-Works-Sigmund-Standard/dp/0393011283Tokarev, A., Phillips, A., Hughes, D., & Irwing, P. (2017). Leader dark traits, workplace bullying, and employee depression: Exploring mediation and the role of the dark core. *Journal of Abnormal Psychology* 126: 911–920. https://psycnet.apa.org/record/2017-49368-007

Tourish, D. (2013). *The Dark Side of Transformational Leadership. A Critical Perspective.* New York: Routledge. https://www.researchgate.net/publication/272890851_Dennis_Tourish_The_Dark_Side_of_Transformational_Leadership_A_Critical_Perspective_New_York_NY_Routledge_2013_252_pages_3995_paperback

U.S. Bureau of Labor Statistic. (2020). *Facts Over Time: Women in the Labor Force.* https://www.bls.gov/opub/reports/womens-databook/2020/home.htm

van Schie, C. C., Jarman, H. L., Huxley, E., & Grenyer, B. F. S. (2020). Narcissistic traits in young people: Understanding the role of parenting and maltreatment. *Borderline Personality Disorder and Emotion Dysregulation* 7. https://bpded.biomedcentral.com/articles/10.1186/s40479-020-00125-7

Verdasca, A. T. (2011). Workplace bullying, power and organizational politics: A study of the Portuguese banking sector. PhD Economic Sociology, Centre of Research in Economic Sociology, Technical University of Lisbon Rua Miguel Lupi. https://socius.rc.iseg.ulisboa.pt/RePEc/soc/wpaper/wp062011.pdf

Wang, L. (2021). The impact of narcissistic leader on subordinates and team followership: Based on "guanxi" perspective. *Frontiers in Psychology* 12: 684380. https://doi.org/10.3389/fpsyg.2021.684380

Washburn, J. J., & Paskar, L. D. (2011). Moving beyond parents in the etiology of narcissistic traits. In: Barry C. T., Kerig P. K., Stellwagen K. K., & Barry T. D. (eds) *Narcissism and Machiavellianism in Youth: Implications for the Development of*

Adaptive and Maladaptive Behavior (pp. 145–157). American Psychological Association. https://doi.org/10.1037/12352-008

Webster, B. D., & Smith, M. B. (2018). The dark triad and organizational citizenship behaviors: The moderating role of high involvement management climate. *Journal of Business and Psychology* 34: 621–635.

Wink, P., & Gough, H. G. (1990). New narcissism scales for the California Psychological Inventory and MMPI. *Journal of Personality Assessment 54(3-4)*: 446–462.

Wirtz, N., & Rigotti, T. (2020). When grandiose meets vulnerable: Narcissism and well-being in the organizational context. *European Journal of Work and Organizational Psychology* 29: 556–569. https://doi.org/10.1080/1359432X.2020.1731474

Wisse, B., Barelds, D., & Rietzschel, E. (2015). How innovative is your employee? The role of employee and supervisor dark triad personality traits in supervisor perceptions of employee innovative behavior. *Personality and Individual Differences* 82: 158–162. 10.1016/j.paid.2015.03.020

Wolven, K. E. (2015). Grandiose and vulnerable narcissism: Where do the emotional difference lies? University of South Carolina Aiken, Psychology Theses 18. https://scholarcommons.sc.edu/cgi/viewcontent.cgi?article=1017&context=aiken_psychology_theses

Xiaohong, X., Fengzhong, L., Fangfang, Z., & Silu, C. (2018). Narcissistic leadership and employees' knowledge sharing: Influence of organizational identification and collectivism. *Social Behavior and Personality* 46: 1317–1330. https://www.sbp-journal.com/index.php/sbp/article/view/7034

Yalch, M., & Levendosky, A. (2019). Influence of betrayal trauma on borderline personality disorder traits. *Journal of Trauma & Dissociation* 20: 392–401. 10.1080/15299732.2019.1572042.

Zajenkowski, M., Maciantowicz, O., Szymaniak, K., & Urban, P. (2018, August 13). Vulnerable and grandiose narcissism are differentially associated with ability and trait emotional intelligence. *Frontiers in Psychology* 9: 1606. https://www.frontiersin.org/articles/10.3389/fpsyg.2018.01606/full

Zhi-Hui, D., Hua-Cheng, L., Lei, Q., & Hua-Qiang, W. (2018). Reluctant to speak? The impact of supervisor narcissism on employee prohibitive voice. *Social Behavior and Personality* 46: 1713–1726. https://www.sbp-journal.com/index.php/sbp/article/view/7233

3 The Narcissistic Leader

Perception, Evaluation, and Research Methodology

Recently, research has emerged into examining narcissism in an organizational framework and the leadership role within an organization. Many people believe that a future leader of an organization must have narcissistic features because narcissistic individuals have personality traits that are generally considered those of a leader by society.

The literature has shown that narcissistic leaders can be either seen positively or negatively; thus, this research considered it necessary to research why such a phenomenon occurs. The traits of narcissistic personality indicate that such individuals can exhibit positive and negative characteristics that can affect the company outcomes and employee's effectiveness. The existing research has already shown the positive and negative results that narcissistic leaders can bring to an organization (Baar, 2015; Braun, 2017; Grijalva et al., 2015; Nevicka et al., 2018). Researchers have also examined how it affects the organization's outcomes and how it affects employees' performance (Grijalva et al., 2015; Nevicka et al., 2018). However, existing research has only given overall general information on this subject, hence the need to test in the presented study how the different types of independent variables, such as the type of leader evaluation, influence the perception of narcissistic leaders in an organization.

The reviewed articles have also stated that the perception of narcissistic leaders influences the outcomes of the organization and the well-being of employees (Galvin, Lange, & Ashforth, 2014; Grijalva et al., 2015; Hart et al., 2017; Mainah & Perkins, 2016; Nevicka et al., 2018; Schyns & Schilling, 2012). Research has indicated that in the company setting, the leaders' assessments were either performed through self-reporting or other-reporting by followers or significant others, which influenced how the narcissistic leader was perceived. This research aimed to show that the narcissistic leader's opinion depends on the forms and subjects of the evaluation.

Research Method

The chosen research examined the organization's narcissistic leaders based on the various forms of leader evaluation. Along with leader evaluation, the proposed study examined the impact of a narcissistic leader

DOI: 10.4324/9781003260646-3

on employee outcomes and leader-employee relations. The research was based on a review of already existing articles found on online databases. The articles chosen for this research are peer-reviewed scholarly articles extracted from the school library using the EBSCO search engine while following precisely design criteria. The articles contained information concerning three main research questions: the forms of narcissistic leader evaluation, the perception of a narcissistic leader in the organization, and the employee outcomes.

The best method to perform the proposed study was the qualitative research method based on existing articles on a given subject. It was conducted in the form of an explanatory case study (Harrison et al., 2017). The research question guiding this study is "How does the type of narcissistic leader evaluation change the perception of a leader in the organization?" The dependent variable in this research was the perception of the narcissistic leader. The independent variable was the type of evaluation of narcissistic leaders that takes two forms: the leaders' self-evaluation and the employees' assessment of narcissistic leaders.

The chosen method was appropriate for this study because there were many articles on the subject of a narcissistic leader in the organization. Therefore, there was no need to research whether narcissistic leaders appeared in organizations and the consequences of having these types of leaders concerning the leader assessment methods. Previous research has also already examined the impact of narcissistic leaders on the organization and employees (Braun, 2017). Therefore, there was no necessity to explore that again. The study's goal was to group the information and describe and explain the causes and consequences of the presented situations to the reader.

As mentioned, the case study was chosen as the appropriate type of research method for this study because, as Harrison et al. (2017) have suggested, it is "a methodology that allowed to investigate and understand several issues in the real world settings" and is used across several disciplines such as education, business, law, health, and social science (p. 1). Thus, this research method did not have well-defined and well-structured protocols; it allowed creating its own. However, the case study's prominent methodologists, R.K. Yin, S.B. Merriam, and R.E. Stake (Yazan, 2015), have established procedures for the case study method. Having this information in mind, a researcher could conduct his protocols while following the procedures that guide researchers to conduct proper case studies. Furthermore, a case study is comprehensive and reduces biases as it is an in-depth investigation of a particular problem, individual, group of people, or event. It means that this study method provides a variety of tools to investigate a case and offers a broader perspective of the problem. At the same time, it eliminates the researcher's bias.

Participants

The topic of the given research paper was the perception of narcissistic leaders in organizations. The study also examined what influence various leader evaluation methods had on how a narcissistic leader was perceived and what impact the narcissistic leader had on their subordinates. This study's research method was the qualitative research design based on already existing articles on the topic. It was conducted in the form of an explanatory case study. Concerning the chosen research design, there were no selected participants for this study. However, there were scrutiny criteria assigned for the articles chosen for this research paper. The criteria concerned the general topic of a narcissistic leader in the organization and detailed criteria concerning each research question.

As mentioned, the proposed research was based on the review of already existing articles about the subject from online databases of the university's library. The articles were peer-reviewed and gathered from scholarly journals from the psychology, economy, and management departments. The materials were selected via strictly designed criteria. The first criterion was to search the EBSCO search engine's online database using keywords linked with the organization's narcissistic leader. The chosen words included "narcissism," "narcissistic leaders," "employee," "follower," "perception of a narcissistic leader," "narcissistic CEO," and many variations of those words. The conducted search presented 350 articles on the chosen subject from 1914 to 2019. The reports followed specific criteria and were divided into three groups. One group consisted of research articles containing information about the perception of narcissistic leaders by the organization (positive and negative). The second group included articles that provided information on the forms of evaluation of narcissistic leaders such as self-reports and others' reports. The third group contained articles with information about the outcome that a narcissistic leader's behavior had on the employees, focusing on the negative impact.

The first criterion concerned the first research question and is the material containing few forms of leader evaluation with the main focus on the leader's self-evaluation and the other-evaluation (the follower's assessment; Galvin, Lange, & Ashforth, 2014; Grijalva et al., 2015; Hart et al., 2017; Nevicka et al., 2018). The following research indicated that in the company setting, the leaders' assessment was either performed through self-reporting or other-reporting by followers or significant others, which influenced the narcissistic leader's perception.

The second criterion, related to the second research question, was that articles should be included that contained data on how narcissistic leaders were viewed in the organization, including both the positive and negative opinions (Baars, 2015; Braun, 2017; Grijalva et al., 2015; Nevicka et al., 2018). It has been noted that through all the reviewed articles, quantitative measures were most commonly used to assess leader narcissism.

The last criterion was that articles should be included that contained information on the outcomes of narcissistic leader behavior on the well-being of employees and the organization (Galvin, Lange, & Ashforth, 2014; Grijalva et al., 2015; Hart et al., 2017; Nevicka et al., 2018; Mainah & Perkins, 2016). This criterion was necessary as the purpose of the review was to describe the relationships between leader narcissism and organizational outcomes.

Instrumentation

Research Protocols

The research protocols were conducted following the written schema, with the specification of each research question.

1 Justification of the research

The research was based on an article review of already existing information on the topic of narcissistic leaders in an organization. It included scholarly articles regarding narcissism, narcissistic personality traits, narcissistic leaders, the perception of narcissism, and forms of evaluation of narcissistic leaders in organizations. This research aimed to examine the opinion about the narcissistic leader in the organization based on the narcissistic leader evaluation method. The study was based on these findings and extended the topic to show that such leaders' perception was linked with the form of assessment and that this impacted the outcomes of such behavior by negatively affecting other employees, especially the lower-level ones. This research method has also expressed that such leaders' narcissistic behavior has a very negative influence on employees of a given organization, causing stress, lack of job motivation, lowering effectiveness and job satisfaction, and in some cases, causing people to resign from work. It means that the literature review went in three directions to answer the following questions.

2 Research questions

The first research question concerned the various techniques used to evaluate narcissistic leaders. The goal was to show that such a leader's perception depended on the methods of leader assessment. The second question investigated the impact that the various forms of narcissistic leader evaluation had on how the leaders were perceived (whether positively or negatively). Based on already existing data, the research also tested the influence that the narcissistic leader had on their subordinates and the outcome of this influence.

3 Research methods

The research method chosen for this study was the literature review of research on narcissistic leaders in organizations. It was performed as a qualitative study in which content analysis was used for data collection.

I followed the content analysis guidelines (Erlingsson & Brysiewicz, 2017) to create valuable data collection criteria. The main rules for inclusion stated that the articles had to be scholarly peer-reviewed articles from academic journals to ensure research quality. The reports were extracted from the University of Southern California database, and the leading search engine used for the study was EBSCO Host. Several sub-engines linked to EBSCO Hosts were also used such as Psychology and Behavioral Science Collection, PsycInfo, PsycArticles (APA), and PubMed.

4 Study population
The articles for the study were gathered from the database of the California Southern University online library. The population of the study was the 350 articles on the subject that were published from 1914 to 2019. The chosen materials had to follow scrutiny criteria to be qualified for the study. Out of all the researched articles, only 33 qualified for the second research question, which was concerning the perception of a narcissistic leader in an organization. For the third research question, concerning outcomes of the narcissistic leader on the employees qualified 38 articles.

5 Questionnaires and other data collection
Concerning the first research question, for the proper data collection, there have been established strict criteria following chosen keywords were "methods of employee evaluation in organizations," "narcissistic leader evaluation methods," "forms of narcissistic leader assessment," "levels of analysis," and other combinations of these words.

Regarding the second research question, about the perception of a narcissistic leader in the organization, articles were chosen if they contained the following containing given keywords: "perception of leaders in an organization," "corporate narcissism," "opinion of the narcissistic leader," and other variations of similar words.

Lastly, for the third research question, the articles had to include the following keywords: "narcissistic leaders and organizational outcome," "influence of narcissistic CEO on employees," "workers outcome," and other variations of these phrases.

Data Collection

This study, on the perception of a narcissistic leader in the organization, used a qualitative research method based on a literature review of existing information on narcissistic leaders in organizations. The articles used for this study were selected carefully from the California Southern University's online library database. The research consists of three research questions; therefore, there were strict and specific criteria assigned to each topic. The main criteria applied to all the questions were that the articles had to be scholarly and peer-reviewed and had to contain the keywords chosen for each question.

Data Analysis

I began the analysis by reviewing the chosen resources and summarizing them in accordance with research question. The research was based on articles extracted from the online database. During the research process, articles were retrieved that contained valuable information on narcissistic employee evaluation in organizational settings. Considering the subject of this research, which was determining how narcissistic leaders are perceived by using self-reports and other reports, I have chosen articles that followed those two requirements. Therefore, the scholarly articles were divided into groups, in which one was articles on self-reporting and the other on other-reporting of narcissistic leaders.

The chosen articles were accepted if they discussed the method of narcissistic leader evaluations used in the organizations. Each of the publications was examined to determine if they fit the three main criteria: discussing self-ratings, the ratings of others, and the articles that contained both methods.

The majority of articles that included the self-rating assessment of the narcissistic leader used the 40-item NPI presented by Raskin and Terry (1988) to evaluate narcissism. The second most commonly used form of narcissistic leader evaluation was the 16-item version of NPI created by Ames and colleagues (Ames et al., 2006). In the other articles, the researchers used the Dark Triad (SD3, Jones & Paulhus, 2014), the Chatterjee Hambrick method (2007), and California Psychology Inventory (CPI; Wink & Gough, 1990).

In the articles that presented the self-ratings of narcissistic leaders, the researchers used the 40-item NPI (Galvin, Waldman, & Balthazard, 2010; Nevicka et al., 2011; Ong et al., 2016), 16-item NPI (De Hoogh, Hartog, & Nevicka, 2015; Foti et al., 2012; Nevicka et al., 2011; Owens et al., 2015), and CPI (Blair, Hoffman, & Helland 2008). The presented articles stated that in their self-ratings, narcissistic leaders tend to see themselves as having positive leadership qualities. It was also correlated with the grandiose narcissism and narcissistic tendency to rate themselves high and dominate others.

Another group of articles used the other-ratings to assess the narcissistic leaders in organizations. These articles have followed the same main methods presented above. Most of these articles used the Gough Adjective Check List (Braun et al., 2016; O'Reilly et al., 2014; Resick et al., 2009) and the prominence of the CEO's photograph in the annual report as the measure of the narcissism of leaders in organizations (Olsen, Dworkis, & Young 2014; Patel & Cooper, 2014; Zhu & Chen, 2015). There was also a group of articles that used the variation of both types of evaluation. It includes a 40-item NPI (Nevicka et al., 2013) and a 16-item NPI (Braun et al., 2016; Mainah & Perkins, 2016). Mainah and Perkins (2016) noticed that narcissistic leaders have a distorted self-image, which correlates with them answering favorably when assessing themselves in self-reports and self-evaluation tests. These tests show that they have a positive self-rating and, therefore, influence how the narcissistic leader behaves (Judge, LePine, & Rich, 2015). However, when the assessment was strictly performed by the narcissistic leader's subordinates, such a leader's perception was negative. This perception was related to positive leader emergence and negative leader effectiveness.

The next aspect of the research paper was to establish the leader-employee outcomes after having determined the perceptions of narcissistic leaders. The chosen articles were screened for this purpose and placed into groups if they contained at least one employee's statement about negative outcomes after being under the supervision of narcissistic leaders. These employee statements included the following words or sentiments: envy, lower job performance, job burnout, low job commitment, stress, depression, decreased prosocial behavior, lower self-esteem, and unwillingness of subordinates to speak out.

The results of the study showed that the perception of the narcissistic leader resulted in specific leader-employer outcomes. It has been verified that negative perception of a narcissistic leader related to their dominant behavior results in lower job performance (Nevicka et al., 2018), lower job commitment (Keller Hansbrough & Jones, 2014), and even job burnout (Nevicka et al., 2018). Research has also noted that such employees felt silenced by their employees (Liao et al., 2017) and highly exploited by them (Campbell et al., 2011). Despite this, many subordinates of narcissistic leaders suffer psychological problems such as stress and even depression (Hua-Qiang, Guang-Lei, & Zhi-Hui 2018; Keller Hansbrough & Jones, 2014) and lower self-esteem (Mainah & Perkins 2016). The subordinates who had a negative perception of their narcissistic leaders claimed to have lower prosocial behavior (Liu et al., 2017).

To limit the research bias at the beginning of the design process, I established strict criteria for selecting the articles. The requirements stated that the articles had to be peer-reviewed scholarly studies that contained information on the subject of the method of leader evaluation, the perception of a narcissistic leader in the organization, and at least one form of leader-employee outcomes. By following the criteria, the research can be retaken by future researchers and replicated. It assures the validity of the study. The research has shown that the perception of a narcissistic leader correlates with how the leader is assessed in such an organization. The correlation indicates that when leaders perform the self-report, they demonstrate that they have a positive opinion of themselves; however, when subordinates perform the evaluation, the perception of leaders is negative.

References

Ames, R., Rose, P., & Anderson, C. (2006). The npi-16 as a short measure of narcissism. *Journal of Research in Personality* 40: 440–450. https://www.sciencedirect.com/science/article/abs/pii/S0092656605000504, https://www.researchgate.net/publication/346797502_Impact_of_narcissistic_leadership_on_employee_work_outcomes_in_banking_sector_of_Pakistan

Baars, S. (2015). Narcissistic leadership. https://docplayer.net/56209673-Narcissistic-leadership.html

Blair, C., Hoffman, B., & Helland, K. (2008). Narcissism in organizations: A multisource appraisal reflects different perspectives. *Human Performance* 21(3): 254–276. https://link.springer.com/chapter/10.1007/978-3-319-60330-8_4

Braun, S. (2017). Leader narcissism and outcomes in organizations: A review at multiple levels of analysis and implications for future research. *Frontiers in Psychology* 8: 773. https://www.frontiersin.org/articles/10.3389/fpsyg.2017.00773/full

Braun, S., Aydin, N., Frey, D., & Peus, C. (2016). Leader narcissism predicts malicious envy and supervisor-targeted counterproductive work behavior – evidence from field and experimental research. *Journal of Business Ethics* 151: 725–741. http://dro.dur.ac.uk/18920

Campbell, K. W., Hoffman, B. J., Campbell, S. M., & Marchisio, G. (2011, December). Narcissism in organizational contexts. *Human Resource Management Review* 21: 268–284. https://digitalcommons.kennesaw.edu/facpubs/1582/

Chatterjee, A., & Hambrick, D. (2007). It's all about me: Narcissistic chief executive officers and their effects on company strategy and performance. *Administrative Science Quarterly* 52: 351–386. https://journals.sagepub.com/doi/abs/10.2189/asqu.52.3.351

De Hoogh, A., Hartog, D., & Nevicka, B. (2015). Gender differences in the perceived effectiveness of narcissistic leaders. *Applied Psychology* 64: 473–498. https://onlinelibrary.wiley.com/doi/abs/10.1111/apps.12015

Erlingsson, C., & Brysiewicz, P. (2017). A hands-on guide to doing content analysis. *African Journal of Emergency Medicine* 7: 93–99. https://www.sciencedirect.com/science/article/pii/S2211419X17300423

Foti, R., Bray, B., Thompson, N., & Allgood, S. (2012). Know thy self, know thy leader: Contributions of a pattern-oriented approach to examining leader perceptions. *The Leadership Quarterly* 23(4): 702–717. https://www.sciencedirect.com/science/article/pii/S1048984312000240

Galvin, B., Lange, D., & Ashforth, B. (2014). Narcissistic organizational identification: Seeing oneself as central to the organization's identity. *Academy of Management Review* 40. https://journals.aom.org/doi/abs/10.5465/amr.2013.0103

Galvin, B. M., Waldman, D., & Balthazard, P. A. (August 2010). Visionary communication qualities as mediators of the relationship between narcissism and attributions of leader charisma. *Personnel Psychology* 63(3): 509–537. https://doi.org/10.1111/j.1744-6570.2010.01179.x

Grijalva, E., Harms, P., Newman, D., Gaddis, B., & Fraley, R. (2015). Narcissism and leadership: A meta-analytic review of linear and nonlinear relationships. *Personnel Psychology* 68: 1–47. https://onlinelibrary.wiley.com/doi/abs/10.1111/peps.12072

Harrison, H., Birks, M., Franklin, R., & Mills, J. (2017). Case study research: Foundations and methodological orientations. *Forum: Qualitative Social Research* 18(1). http://www.qualitative-research.net/index.php/fqs/article/view/2655/4079

Hart, W., Adams, J., Burton, A., & Tortoriello, G. (2017). Narcissism and self-presentation: Profiling grandiose and vulnerable Narcissists' self-presentation tactic use. *Personality and Individual Differences* 104: 48–57. https://www.sciencedirect.com/science/article/abs/pii/S0191886916308121. https://link.springer.com/article/10.1007/s10551-012-1296-4

Hua-Qiang, W., Guang-Lei, Z., Zhi-Hui, D., & Zhi-Hui, C. (2018). How supervisor narcissism contributes to employee silence: Roles of negative anticipations and leader–member exchange. *Social Behavior and Personality* 46(4): 653–666. https://www.sbp-journal.com/index.php/sbp/article/view/6815

Jones, D., & Paulhus, D. (2014). Introducing the Short Dark Triad (SD3): A brief measure of dark personality traits. *Assessment* 21: 28–41. https://journals.sagepub.com/doi/10.1177/1073191113514105

Judge, T., LePine, J., & Rich, B. (2015). Loving yourself abundantly: Relationship of the narcissistic personality to self- and other perceptions of workplace deviance, leadership, and task and contextual performance. *Journal of Applied Psychology* 91(4): 762–776. https://asu.pure.elsevier.com/en/publications/loving-yourself-abundantly-relationship-of-the-narcissistic-perso

Keller Hansbrough, T., & Jones, G. (2014). Inside the Minds of Narcissists: How narcissistic leaders' cognitive processes contribute to abusive supervision. *Zeitschrift für Psychologie* 222(4): 214–220. https://econtent.hogrefe.com/doi/10.1027/2151-2604/a000188

Liao, S., Zhou, X., Guo, Z., & Li, Z. (2017). How does leader narcissism influence employee voice: The attribution of leader impression management and leader-member exchange. *International Journal of Environmental Research and Public Health* 16: 1819. https://www.mdpi.com/1660-4601/16/10/1819

Liu, H., Chiang, J., Fehr, R., Xu, M., & Wang, S. (2017). How do leaders react when treated unfairly? Leader narcissism and self-interested behavior in response to unfair treatment. *Journal of Applied Psychology* 102(11): 1590–1599. https://insights.ovid.com/applied-psychology/japsy/2017/11/000/leaders-react-when-treated-unfairly-leader/6/00004565

Mainah, F., & Perkins, V. (2016). Narcissism in organizational leadership. http://www.docdatabase.net/more-narcissism-in-organizational-leadership-fredah-mainah--1327285.html

Nevicka, B., De Hoogh, A. H., Van Vianen, A. E., & Ten Velden, F. S. (2013). Uncertainty enhances the preference for narcissistic leaders. *European Journal of Social Psychology* 43: 370–380. https://www.narcis.nl/publication/RecordID/oai%3Adare.uva.nl%3Apublications%2F84d8e93b-f2a0-41f4-9475-20a793aeb194

Nevicka, B., Van Vianen, A., De Hoogh, A., & Voorn, B. (2018). Narcissistic leaders: An asset or a liability? Leader visibility, follower responses, and group-level absenteeism. *Journal of Applied Psychology* 103: 703–723. https://dare.uva.nl/personal/search?identifier=3206d78e-0bdd-43d2-9ba5-98c5d2cd6157

Nevicka, B., Velden, F., Hoogh, A., & Vianen, A. (2011). Reality at odds with perceptions: Narcissistic leaders and group performance. *Psychological Science* 22: 1259–1264. https://journals.sagepub.com/doi/10.1177/0956797611417259

Olsen, K., Dworkis, K. K., & Young, S. M. (2014). CEO narcissism and accounting: A picture of profits. *Journal of Management Accounting Research* 26(2): 243–267. https://papers.ssrn.com/sol3/papers.cfm?abstract_id=2115067

Ong, C., Roberts, R., Calum, A., Woodman, T., & Akehurst, S. (2016). The leadership is sinking: A temporal investigation of narcissistic leadership. *Journal of Personality* 84: 237–247. https://onlinelibrary.wiley.com/doi/abs/10.1111/jopy.12155

O'Reilly, C., Doerr, B., Caldwell, D., & Chatman, J. (2014). Narcissistic CEOs and executive compensation. *The Leadership Quarterly* 25: 218–231. https://www.sciencedirect.com/science/article/pii/S1048984313000805

Owens, B., Wallace, A., & Waldman, D. (2015). Leader narcissism and follower outcomes: The counterbalancing effect of leader humility. *Journal of Applied Psychology* 100: 1203–1213. https://asu.pure.elsevier.com/en/publications/leader-narcissism-and-follower-outcomes-the-counterbalancing-effe

Patel, P., & Cooper, D. (2014). The harder they fall, the faster they rise: Approach and avoidance focus in narcissistic CEOs. *Strategic Management Journal* 35: 1528–1540. https://onlinelibrary.wiley.com/doi/10.1002/smj.2162

Paulhus, D. L., & Williams, K. M. (2002). The Dark Triad of personality: Narcissism, Machiavellianism, and psychopathy. *Journal of Research in Personality* 36(6): 556–563. https://academic.microsoft.com/paper/1982777740/citedby/search?q=The%20Dark%20Triad%20of%20personality%3A%20Narcissism%2C%20Machiavellianism%2C%20and%20psychopathy&qe=RId%253D1982777740&f=&orderBy=0

Raskin, R., & Shaw, R. (1988). Narcissism and the use of personal pronouns. *Journal of Personality* 56: 393–404. http://onlinelibrary.wiley.com/doi/10.1111/j.1467-6494.1988.tb00892.x/abstract

Raskin, R., & Terry, H. (1988). A principal-components analysis of the Narcissistic Personality Inventory and further evidence of its construct validity. *Journal of Personality and Social Psychology* 54: 890–902. http://dx.doi.org/10.1037/0022-3514.54.5.890

Resick, C., Whitman, D., Weingarden, S., & Hiller, N. (2009). The bright-side and the dark-side of CEO personality: Examining core self-evaluations, narcissism, transformational leadership, and strategic influence. *Journal of Applied Psychology* 94(6): 1365–1381. https://www.sciencedirect.com/science/article/pii/S0191886912000530

Schyns, J., & Schilling, B. (2012). How bad are the effects of bad leaders? A meta-analysis of destructive leadership and its outcomes. *The Leadership Quarterly* 24: 138–158. https://www.sciencedirect.com/science/article/pii/S1048984312000872

Wink, P., & Gough, H. G. (1990). New narcissism scales for the California Psychological Inventory and MMPI. *Journal of Personality Assessment* 54(3–4): 446–462. https://doi.org/10.1207/s15327752jpa5403&4_2

Yazan, B. (2015). Three approaches to case study methods in education: Yin, Merriam, and Stake. *The Qualitative Report* 20: 134–152. https://nsuworks.nova.edu/tqr/vol20/iss2/12/

Zhu, D. H., & Chen, G. (2015). CEO narcissism and the impact of prior board experience on corporate strategy. *Administrative Science Quarterly* 60: 31–65. https://doi.org/10.1177/0001839214554989

4 Narcissistic Leaders within Organizations

Employee Evaluation versus Perception

This research discusses the perception of a narcissistic leader in an organization. The study is important because it shows that the perception of narcissistic leaders varies depending on the form of leader evaluation. To closely examine the problem, three research questions have been raised. The first research question pertains to the methods of narcissistic leader evaluation used in the organization. The second research question concerns the perception of a narcissistic leader in the organization and how it depends on leader evaluation methods. The third research question measures employee-leader outcomes. The proposed study examines the correlation between how the narcissistic leader is evaluated and the perception of such a leader in the organization. Its goals are to show that through the self-evaluation, the ratings of narcissistic leaders are much higher than the employee or other-evaluations. The research also points out that how a narcissistic leader is perceived is connected with the employee-leader relationship, which negatively influences workers' outcomes.

Trustworthiness

Credibility

The research was based on the literature review of existing data on the organization's narcissistic leader. The study was conducted as qualitative research with the intent to use the content analysis for collected data. There have been proper criteria for this study, which states that chosen articles have to be scholarly peer-reviewed ones retrieved from academic journals. Those articles were extracted from the online library of the California Southern University. The population of the study was the 350 researched articles on the presented subject that ranged from 1914 to 2019. The chosen articles had to follow scrutiny criteria in order to be qualified for the study. Of all the researched articles, only 33 qualified for the second research question, and 38 for the third research question. Such action assured research credibility.

DOI: 10.4324/9781003260646-4

Transferability

For the following research, I chose a case study to gather and analyze data. A case study, as an in-depth investigation of a particular problem, individual, group of people, or event, is comprehensive and reduces bias. Thus, this study method provides a variety of tools to investigate a case and offers a broader perspective of the problem. At the same time, it eliminates research bias. Therefore, a case study can be used to bring together similar situations, populations, or phenomena.

Dependability

To limit the research bias at the beginning of the design process, I established strict criteria for selecting the articles. The requirements stated that the articles had to be peer-reviewed scholarly studies that contained information on the subject of the method of leader evaluation, the perception of a narcissistic leader in the organization, and at least one form of leader-employee outcome. The study contains scrutiny criteria for the article collection for each research question that allows the research to be validated by future researchers and replicated.

Confirmability

The research results were solely based on the results coming from the articles reviewed according to the chosen criteria. A protocol was written for each research question to establish research confirmability. The protocol consisted of justifying the research, research question, research methods, study population and questionnaires, and other data collection methods.

Context for Research Questions

The study investigated the perception of a narcissistic leader in an organization using two methods of leader assessment. For the ways of leader assessment, the researcher has chosen the self-rating (self-reports) and others' ratings (reports). I believe that there is a connection between leadership evaluation forms and the narcissistic leader's perception. While researching the topic, I came upon various side effects of narcissistic leadership on employees and organizations. Therefore, the outcomes of narcissistic leaders on their employees are also to be examined in this research. Considering the above, three research questions have been established.

The first research question concerns the various techniques of narcissistic leader evaluation. I wanted to examine whether leader evaluation methods impact how a leader is perceived by their subordinates or coworkers. The goal is to show whether such a leader's opinion depends on the leader assessment methods and, if so, to what extent. As evaluation methods are an essential part of the research, the study's author chose self and others' ratings.

The second question investigates the impact that the various forms of narcissistic leader evaluation have on how a leader is perceived. For the research, I categorized a narcissistic leader's perception as positive or negative. This research hypothesizes that the perception of a narcissistic leader relies on self or other ratings of the leader. The researcher also plans to show that the opinion of narcissistic leaders ranges from positive to negative depending on the method of evaluation used.

Based on already existing data, the research also tested the influence that the narcissistic leader has on their subordinates and the outcome of this influence. Existing studies on the topic of a narcissistic leader in an organization have identified that there are many side effects of such leaders' behavior on their subordinates and coworkers. The current research goal is to demonstrate and group the outcomes of narcissistic leaders' actions on their followers. It also aims to show that narcissistic behavior mostly harms employees and the organization.

Participants and Location

The topic of the presented research is the perception of the narcissistic leader in an organization. Three research questions were designed to examine the studied phenomena. The study was based on existing literature on a narcissistic leader in organizations. Therefore, there are no specific participants or location of the research. However, particular criteria were designed to narrow down the search area and provide the most accurate results for this study's topic. The criteria were composed separately for each research question to bring out the best results.

The articles chosen for this paper were retrieved from the online database of the California Southern University Library. Peer-reviewed articles from scholarly journals on psychology, economy, and management were selected. Additional criteria were created to assure the accuracy of the research. First, the author searched the online database of the EBSCO search engine using the following keywords: "narcissism," "narcissistic leaders," "employee," "follower," "perception of a narcissistic leader," "narcissistic CEO," and many variations of these words. After applying the keywords, 350 articles relevant to the chosen topic of the presented research paper were identified and dated from 1914 to 2018. Of these articles, 38 met the criteria for inclusion. In the next step, the extracted articles were categorized into three selected groups separated by the research questions. The first group followed the criteria for the first research question: the perception of a narcissistic leader (positive and negative). The next group of articles corresponded with the second research question: the forms of evaluation of narcissistic leaders such as self-reports and others' reports. The last group contained articles with information about the outcome that a narcissistic leader's behavior had on the employees, focusing on the negative impact of a leader.

Of the chosen articles, I focused on the forms of leader evaluation with attention paid to the leader's self-evaluation and the other-evaluation (the follower's assessment; Galvin, Lange, & Ashforth, 2014; Grijalva et al., 2015; Hart et al., 2017; Nevicka et al., 2018). The following research indicates that in a company setting, the leaders' assessment is either performed through self-reporting or other-reporting by followers or other subordinates, thus influencing the narcissistic leader's perception.

For the second research question, the chosen articles include data presenting how narcissistic leaders are viewed in the organization, including the positive and negative opinions (Baars, 2015; Braun, 2017; Grijalva et al., 2015; Nevicka et al., 2018). It has been noted that quantitative measures are generally the most common approaches used to assessing leader narcissism.

Lastly, the articles contained information about the outcomes of narcissistic leader behavior on the well-being of employees and the organization (Galvin, Lange, & Ashforth, 2014; Grijalva et al., 2015; Hart et al., 2017; Nevicka et al., 2018; Mainah & Perkins, 2016). This criterion was necessary as the purpose of the review was to describe the relationships between leader narcissism and organizational outcomes.

Results Research Question 1

The presented research's primary focus is to examine the perception of the narcissistic leader in an organization. To verify the perception of a narcissistic leader in the organization, the author reviewed several articles that met the criteria requirements for the three research questions. The presented part of the dissertation presents the research findings for Research Question 1 on narcissistic leader evaluation methods.

Methods of Narcissistic Leader Evaluation

Throughout the research, it has been shown that in the previous study, the author has used various forms of assessment of narcissistic leaders. Studies have applied ready-made evaluation forms that have been attested and used widely to assess the level of narcissism in an individual. Such evaluation forms are the 40-item narcissistic personality inventory (NPI) (Galvin, Waldman, & Balthazard, 2010; Hart et al., 2017; Nevicka et al., 2011; Ong at al., 2016), the 16-item version of the NPI (De Hoogh, Hartog, & Nevicka, 2015; Foti et al., 2012; Nevicka et al., 2011; Owens, Wallace, & Waldman, 2015), the Dark Triad, prominence of CEO photograph in annual reports and press releases, the use of the first-person singular pronouns in interviews (Chatterjee & Hambrick, 2007), and California Psychology Inventory (Blair, Hoffman, & Helland, 2008).

Others' Reports

The crucial aspect of the current research is to evaluate a narcissistic leader using self and others' reports. The study has found that there is a significant difference in the perception of a narcissistic leader when related to leader evaluation. The assessments of narcissistic leader performed by others or, in other words, the other's evaluation or reports give the employees and coworkers of these leaders a chance to give feedback on the leader. The followers could thus state their opinions, especially when the questionnaires were conducted anonymously. It has been noticed that there are other elements, such as the time of the evaluation or the relations between the leader and follower, that impact the perception of such a leader.

In their study, Galvin, Waldman, and Balthazard (2010) noticed that the reports by others of narcissistic leaders, although mostly negative, may depend on when the assessments were performed. If the evaluation was performed at the beginning of a narcissistic leader's or worker's employment at the organization, the assessment resulted in positive feedback because coworkers or subordinates were astounded by the leader's performance. This feedback is related to the positive attributes of narcissistic individuals such as charisma, passion for their job, and ability to take risks. Grijalva et al. (2015) term these factors leader emergence, which describes a state in which a newly employed person wants to present their best attributes and impress their colleagues at the new job. As Grijalva et al. (2015) have discussed, this is also related to the narcissistic leader's employment length. The longer the narcissist works in an organization, the more their negative features are visible.

Schilling and Schyns (2015) came to a similar conclusion concerning narcissistic leader emergence. Over time, the authors pointed out that such an individual's effectiveness decreases and they are perceived as restrictive and counterproductive (Schilling & Schyns, 2015). The narcissistic leader is no longer capable of pretending and hiding their negative side. Nevertheless, the others' reports are more reliable than self-reports; thus, they actually evaluate the job effectiveness of the narcissistic leader, which, as mentioned, decreases over time.

Carlson, Vazire, and Oltmanns (2011) called it the first impression activity, it occurred when a narcissistic leader shows their positive traits to gain acceptance and create a good impression the "first impression activity." In three separate trials, one pertaining to the leaders' acquaintance and close friends, the other to new acquaintances, and the last to coworkers, Carlson, Vazire, and Oltmanns (2011) concluded that narcissistic leaders have an insight that they have an excellent first impression that deteriorates over time. Carlson, Vazire, and Oltmanns (2011) also noted that coworkers perceived their leaders in a less favorable manner than the leader perceived themselves when completing a survey.

Baars (2015) has also noticed that when the evaluation of the narcissistic leader is performed by close others, such as family members or friends, the narcissistic leader most likely will receive positive feedback. As Baars (2015) claimed, such feedback is not objective because it is given by people related to the narcissistic leader and thus might be influenced by the leader. In this case, the family members or close friends may want to protect their narcissistic spouse's flawless image or may fear the narcissist's anger and thus give them good ratings.

The narcissistic leader's evaluation was also introduced in the study conveyed by Owens, Wallace, and Waldman (2015). The authors used Resick et al.'s (2009) NPI to do so. The questionnaire included adjectives typical of narcissists: arrogant, assertive, boastful, proud, egotistical, self-centered, show-off, and temperamental. Through a survey sent out to workers via email, employees had to rate their leader using this scale. The research showed that employees ranked their narcissistic CEOs very high on almost all of the mentioned adjectives.

Sosik, Chun, and Zhu (2014) have also performed a study based on others' reports. They surveyed employees in multiple industries who experienced a leader-follower relationship in their working careers. The research explained that the others' reports were not favorable to narcissistic leaders unless the leaders had a high level of constructive or charismatic leadership. When a narcissistic individual showed signs of destructive leadership, the followers had an adverse opinion of such a leader. The surveyed participants were significantly vocal about their perception of the narcissistic leader because the survey was voluntary and anonymous.

Nevertheless, another form of others' reports was used in research performed by Chatterjee and Hambrick (2007). The researchers used the prominence of the CEO's photograph in annual reports and the CEO's prominence in press releases to measure the outcome of a narcissistic leader in an organization. The authors found that such a leader was positively related to a company's strategy; however, their performance within the company was no better than the leaders at the same level who were not narcissists. Similarly, Zhu and Chen (2015) use the same narcissist evaluation technique as Chatterjee and Hambrick (2007); however, they measure the perception of narcissistic CEOs and the impact of the prior perception of such a leader on new directors. The authors indicated that narcissists strive for external affirmation; therefore, they are prone to hire team members with highly similar personal values and attitudes. However, when a director has the opposite values, the cooperation between them and the CEO is hindered.

Self-Reports

The study also presents that, in some cases, researchers used self-ratings of narcissistic leaders to evaluate their performance in an organization.

Hart et al. (2017) reported in the online review of 264 academic participants about the relation of grandiose narcissism and self-presentation that narcissists always present themselves in a positive light. It was a self-report or self-presentation. Such self-perception measures lack objectivity; thus, narcissists failed to see any faults in themselves. In his study, Carlson, Vazire, and Oltmanns (2011) applied multiple perception examinations, such as that of the first impression activity, and self-perception measures of participants to examine whether narcissists are aware of the negative aspects of their personality. His study showed that narcissists do not have insight into their negative character features, which was visible on the test results. This indicates that narcissists speak highly of themselves most of the time, and the test results will always be in their favor.

Foti et al. (2012) investigated the leaders' perception of themselves concerning the ideal leader's pattern. The authors conducted a study based on latent profile analysis to describe the self-leader and the ideal leader. The research verified four types of self-leader characteristics (prototypical, laissez-faire, narcissistic, anti-prototypical) and similar features of ideal leaders. The results of those studies show that individuals expressing the prototypical and laissez-faire traits perceive the ideal leader as similar to themselves. However, the narcissistic and anti-prototypical leaders had different opinions of the ideal leader traits than themselves.

Martin, Cote, and Woodruff (2016) examined in her study that parental income levels impact self-rated narcissism. They conducted a study on American soldiers and nominated their followers and indicated that soldiers from families with higher income levels expressed more narcissistic traits and perceived themselves as superior as opposed to others. The authors proved that there is a link between an individual's socioeconomic situation and their level of narcissism.

In conclusion, the research results demonstrate that when self-reports are used as a method of leader evaluation, they proved to be subjective and did not represent the actual perception of such a leader in the organization because they were one-sided opinion. The studies have also found that the evaluation of narcissistic leaders performed by other varies over time. The more subordinates were able to see their leader's work performance, the less favorable the opinion they had of their leader. This indicates that the leader's effectiveness deteriorates over time.

Results Research Question 2

Perception of a Narcissistic Leader

The second research question of the study on the topic of perception of a narcissistic leader in an organization concerned the actual opinion such a leader's has among his subordinates and coworkers. This study hypothesized that opinion about narcissistic leaders can either be positive or negative and this is related to the narcissistic leader's evaluation methods. The results for Research Question 1 indicated that the opinion of the leader depends on the technique of narcissistic leader evaluation. The research showed that when the narcissistic leader was assessed, whether through self or others' ratings, the assessment was both positive and negative.

Positive Perception

The favorable perception of a narcissistic leader is related to the methods of assessment of such a leader. Judge, LePine, and Rich (2006) examined the difference in a narcissistic leader's perception through an empirical study of self and other reports. The study revealed that narcissists express a favorable opinion of their leadership, whereas subordinates have mixed perceptions of it. Even as one study has shown that the impression others have of such a leader is positive, this perception was still less positive than the self-ratings. However, the main results showed a weak relationship between narcissistic leaders and their followers, leading to such individuals being negatively perceived.

The CEO or leader can possess both positive and negative attributes of a narcissistic personality. Galvin, Lange, and Ashforth (2014) examined the relationship between the nature of charismatic and narcissistic leadership. The authors have pointed out that aspects such as socialized vision, which are characteristic of a charismatic leader and of vision boldness, are common to narcissistic individuals. This study's findings presented that leader narcissism is negatively related to socialized vision; thus, a narcissist cannot engage with others' higher-order needs. Instead, such individuals tend to impose a bold vision of their own. Therefore, narcissistic leaders lose the favor of their employees because they are not team players.

Foti et al. (2012) examined the relationship between leadership perception and the method of leader evaluation. They surveyed 491 college students who had some previous leadership experience on their self and exemplary leadership and how they rated their narcissism and leadership self-efficacy. They found that narcissistic individuals presented themselves as narcissistic leaders with an indication of high intelligence, dedication to work, and some degree of tyranny. This shows that narcissists perceive themselves rightly and refute the undesirable qualities of their personality.

Braun (2017) has also investigated how narcissistic leaders are perceived through a literature review of 121 articles and quantitative measures of a narcissistic leader using self and others' ratings. The author concluded that narcissists tend to ascribe themselves the good leader's attributes while evaluating their work. However, when their followers performed the assessment, their perception was negative and pointed out less desirable features of their leaders' character.

Braun et al. (2016) performed a study on college students in Germany. The participants were introduced to a questionnaire on the relationship between the leader narcissist and the followers' envy. Braun et al.'s (2016) study results found that many narcissistic leader's followers negatively perceive their superiors, and their emotions range from frustration to an inclination for aggressive acts toward the leader. The authors hypothesized that followers confronted with narcissistic leaders responded with high levels of malicious envy.

Mainah and Perkins (2016) noticed that narcissistic leaders have a distorted self-image, which correlates with them giving favorable answers on the self-reports and self-evaluation tests. Their perception causes them to have a positive self-rating and therefore leads to the positive measures of perception of the narcissistic leader. Therefore, self-reports are not considered reliable sources of leader assessment, although they are an excellent measure of narcissistic traits of the narcissists.

Narcissistic leaders can also be perceived positively by their followers due to their social networking and social media activities. Such leaders are known as great performers who desire to be admired by others; therefore, they continuously extend their network of followers and possible clients. This works well for the business that they lead. In their research on narcissism, Sedikides and Campbell (2017) pointed out the sociocultural aspect of narcissistic leaders. The authors stated that generally, narcissism is positively related to various online social networking activities both in Western cultures and in Eastern (e.g., Chinese, Pakistani) cultures (Sedikides & Campbell, 2017).

Negative Perception

The topic of narcissistic leaders and the followers' victimization was also examined by Nevicka et al. (2018). It has been noticed in the multi-sourced field study that narcissistic leaders have personality traits that predispose them to abusive behavior toward their subordinates. The results indicated that employees under such a leader likely had a negative opinion of their manager. Nevicka et al. (2018) also mentioned that the subordinates' perception of the narcissistic leader worsened even more when the subordinates expressed low self-esteem; thus, they were more sensitive to leaders' abuse. On the contrary, the authors pointed out that employees with higher self-esteem are less subject to the abuse of narcissistic leaders and, therefore, perceived them in a more positive light.

The researchers also examined the topic of narcissistic leaders through the prism of the dark and bright sides of their personality. As Campbell et al. (2011) stated, narcissists can be either good, evil, or both. Thus, as mentioned in the study, some narcissists are considered great leaders due to their charisma, vision, passion, and innovations. These features are typical of narcissistic individuals and are evident at the beginning of narcissist's career in an organization. Campbell et al. (2011) pointed out that the coworkers and subordinates of a narcissistic leader often perceive the leader to be abusive and demanding. They see the leader as an entitled individual who believes they deserve special treatment and credit for their work.

De Hoogh, Hartog, and Nevicka (2015) went further than others when examining the perception of a narcissistic leader in an organization and analyzed it from a gender perspective. Through a study performed on 145 leaders and subordinates dyads, the authors found out that female leaders were perceived as less productive than male leaders. The findings also demonstrated that the correlation of non-female gender qualities, such as arrogance, and lack of stereotypical gender traits, such as kindness, in female narcissists positioned them as a threat to their male colleagues. This precedence was even more visible when examining the ratings performed by male subordinates, while female responders expressed no gender bias in their evaluations of a narcissistic leader.

Carlson, Vazire, and Oltmanns (2011) also contributed to the research with their study on clinical and subclinical narcissism. The research results indicated that narcissistic individuals understood that others saw them as worse than what the narcissists think of themselves. Furthermore, if the narcissists did have an insight into their personality, they perceived themselves as arrogant and ignorant. This indicates that narcissists are aware of their destructive personality traits; however, they tend to ignore them publicly and speak only positively of them.

Rosenthal and Pittinsky (2006) added in their research that there was a minimal correlation between sociocultural aspects and narcissistic leaders. They expressed that although a society as a whole might have shown more or less self-centered behavior (e.g., American vs. Chinese society), the decision to choose a narcissist as a leader was not restricted to a particular country, ideology, or political party. As the authors discussed, some of the world's best-known leaders with negative narcissistic personality traits, such as Saddam Hussein, Mao Zedong, or Ronald Regan, came from different countries (Rosenthal & Pittinsky 2006).

The results showed that the perception of a narcissistic leader is either positive or negative. It also presented that narcissists tend to ascribe to positive features to themselves while evaluating their work as a leader. Nevertheless, that perception significantly changed when employees were asked to assess their leader; thus, their evaluation was based on their weak relationship with the leader and their less desirable features.

Results Research Question 3

Outcomes of a Narcissistic Leader in an Organization

The research results presented that a narcissistic individual's negative characteristics impact their relationship with their coworkers and subordinates and drastically influence employee outcomes. Researchers have noted a variety of adverse outcomes that narcissistic leaders have on their employees. They were divided into the emotional and psychological as well as attitude toward the job.

Psychological Problems

In their study on the correlation between leadership effectiveness, transformational leadership, leadership emergence, and narcissism, Grijalva et al. (2015) showed that leadership effectiveness significantly changed from good to worse over time. Over time, leadership effectiveness becomes negative and employees lose their motivation at work. Tokarev et al. (2017) added that narcissistic leaders tend to bully their subordinates at work. Employees associated workplace bullying with narcissism and psychopathy of their abusive leaders. Excessive bullying causes emotional and psychological distress among employees, which, in the end, leads to depression for over 20% of employees.

Workplace bullying can be institutionalized and begins with the bullies' narcissistic need for recognition and success while ending with a toxic and demoralizing work environment. The study presented by Seigner et al. (2007) shows that in one group of over 300 Irish workers, researchers learned that bullies were more competitive, assertive, concerned with their own success, and aggressive than non-bullies. All those characteristics are associated with narcissism. In addition, the authors stated that bullying is a form of proactive aggression initiated by the narcissist's exploitativeness. Narcissistic leaders use bullying tactics such as taking credit for work, withholding information, feeding misinformation, and sabotage being the most common (Seigner et al., 2007). Paulhus and Williams (2002) discovered that a correlation between bullying and narcissism could be predicted in childhood. In other words, children scoring high in narcissism were more likely to exhibit indirect bullying behaviors than those scoring low.

Another critical study explicitly focused on corporate psychopaths and workplace bullying (Boddy, 2014). The researchers noticed that when corporate psychopaths are present at work, the bullying incidents are significantly higher than when corporate psychopaths are not present (Boddy, 2014). Babiak and Hare (2006) concluded in their work that this is in line with the findings that 29% of corporate psychopaths are bullies. In addition, in organizations led by a corporate psychopath, employees have reported significant levels of dissatisfaction with the company's treatment of and concern for its employees (Babiak & Hare, 2006). Paulhus and Williams (2002) stated in their research that due to the strong correlation between narcissism with psychopathy and Machiavellianism, along with the fact that bullies exhibit many traits associated with narcissism, it can be posited there is a relationship between narcissism and bullying.

Likewise, in his research Schilling and Schyns (2015) presented a correlation between toxic or destructive behaviors and workplace bullying at the supervisory and management levels. It has also shown a relationship when looking specifically at the top leader. The behavioral traits closely associated with narcissism significantly impact companies' culture on bullying. It translates to leadership behaviors that emphasize the fulfillment of personal needs without regard to the impact on others or the organization (Rosenthal & Pittinsky, 2006). It means that these behaviors can result in an organizational culture that condones bullying behaviors. It has also been noticed that bullying by narcissistic leaders negatively impacts employees' well-being. Olive and Cangemi (2015) suggested victims of bullying by a narcissistic leader can be afflicted with anxiety, depression, irritability, and sleeping and eating disorders. More extreme cases can result in suicide, homicide, and Post-Traumatic Stress Disorder (PTSD). Additionally, employees' self-esteem is diminished. It is reduced to the Safety Level (fear) on Maslow's Hierarchy of Needs (Maslow, 1970); thus, they believe that the organization does not care about them as human beings.

Hua-Quiang et al. (2018) added in the research that a significant number of employees who worked under the supervision of a narcissistic leader suffered from various psychological issues. In the three-wave survey among 292 employees in three Chinese companies, they had examined the relations between narcissistic supervisors and employees and found that employees most frequently experienced stress and depression. The authors also pointed out that alongside the psychological issues on individuals, there was a noticeable impact on the organization. The workers encountered lower self-esteem, trust, and job commitment and satisfaction. As the authors mentioned, this is related to the changing quality of the leader-member exchange (LMX) relationship.

Other researchers also noticed that employees working for narcissistic leaders suffer from significant distress. According to Keller Hansbrough and Jones (2014), the most common issues that subordinates face are emotional distress, a diminished sense of well-being, and job tension. As a result of the abusive treatment, employees have lower job commitment and satisfaction and increased intention to quit.

Job Commitment and Performance

Researchers have also examined the impact of leader narcissism on their employees' job commitment and performance. Owens, Wallace, and Waldman (2015) explored the topic by surveying a large health insurance company's leaders and followers. The study found that leader narcissism was related to their humility. At the same time, leaders who were narcissistic and humble were perceived by the employees in a much brighter light, and the employees had positive job outcomes and commitments. Employees also felt encouraged to work harder. Instead, those leaders who lack humility were perceived as less competent and this negatively impacted the subordinates' work performance. Furthermore, employees' attitudinal and behavioral motivation significantly dropped as leaders take credit for their subordinates' work.

Researchers have also noticed that leader narcissism impacts an employee's organizational outcomes. Liao et al. (2017) examined the correlation between the narcissistic leader and employee outcomes related to leader-member exchange and employee willingness to speak up. The study was performed among workers of two state-owned companies in China. The results showed that leader narcissism impacted the quality of LMX by reducing it. Therefore, the subordinates felt silenced and unable to voice their concerns. The silencing of employees is more likely to occur in collectivistic countries like China, where the leader-member relationship is weak. Narcissistic leaders tend to focus on themselves, and subordinates feel less supported, respected, and trusted. As a result, the employees' job commitment and proactive behavior dropped significantly.

Narcissistic behaviors of leaders might impact their followers' trust in them and the company as well. These leaders often seek glory and praise for their or their team achievements, which results in unethical behavior associated with credit taking and bragging about jobs performed by others; this behavior leads followers to distrust leaders. Hua-Quiang et al. (2018) mentioned that employees felt this situation to be unjust and to show a lack of regard for their hard work, which thus lowered job satisfaction. As followed, their job performance, and commitment decreased.

Nevicka et al. (2018) went even further in their research, stating that narcissistic leaders could negatively impact their followers especially if the leaders were dominant and implemented abusive supervision. Such supervision was expressed through verbal and non-verbal behavior rather than physical contact. Nevicka and colleagues (2018) noticed that abusive supervision has terrible consequences on employees because it causes job burnout and lowers performance. Over time, this is harmful to the entire organization.

Credit taking and excessive exploitativeness of employees is another negative effect of narcissistic leaders on employees. Campbell et al. (2011) presented in the research that through abusive supervision, narcissistic leaders exploited their workers with scrutiny and attention to detail when assessing the employees' work and with a constant expectation that their employees would achieve high goals. Keller Hansbrough and Jones (2014) noticed that taking credit for others' work caused tension between workers and narcissistic leaders. Employees felt undervalued and deprived of the well-deserved appreciation for their hard work and commitment. As follows, their commitment to work decreased.

Chatterjee and Hambrick (2007) have examined the issue of narcissistic leaders and their impact on company performance and strategy. They performed a study on 111 CEOs of computer hardware and software companies. Their research showed that narcissistic leaders express overconfidence, grandiose strategic actions, and extreme risk-taking behavior, which seems beneficial for the company's functioning but over time negatively impacts performance. The researchers stated (Chatterjee & Hambrick, 2007) that narcissistic CEOs were the cause of many fluctuations in the company's performance ranging from very high to extremely low, which caused instability. One of the consequences of this instability includes the relocation of resources or the unexpected failure of a line of businesses, which can result in loss of employment and massive layoffs.

The unpredictable actions of narcissistic leaders, especially CEOs, can significantly contribute to the business's rise or fall. In their research on several Fortune 500 companies, Olsen, Dworkis, and Young (2014) found that businesses led by narcissistic CEOs were more likely to engage in tax sheltering, tax avoidance, and implemented fewer tax policies in the office. These factors are related to the narcissistic personality traits of a CEO. Such individuals believe they are above the law and therefore are not obliged to pay taxes. Their sense of superiority and multifaceted personality often ensure that narcissistic individuals engage in questionable behaviors, which poses risks to the company itself. Their actions also adversely affect the company's financial performance, due to their incompetent executive decisions that are motivated by a desire for superiority and fame.

The narcissistic leader's influence on subordinates and organizations' outcome have also been viewed through the prism of the 2008 economic crisis. Narcissists are known as individuals who often engage in risky decisions and behavior in critical situations. As mentioned by Patel and Cooper (2014), during the pre-crisis period of 2007, companies governed by narcissistic CEOs suffered from significant financial decline. The authors of the study noticed a correlation between narcissistic personality and lower avoidance motivation of those CEOs. Nevertheless, the same CEOs had strong approach motivation focused on achieving desirable outcomes. This means that narcissistic leaders knew how to increase company performance in the post-crisis period. According to Patel and Cooper (2014), a narcissistic leader's behavior could greatly benefit an organization but only in the post-crisis period; otherwise, their inability to predict and prepare for a crisis can put the company at significant financial risk.

There are also other negative outcomes on the organization of a narcissistic leader related to bullying. Bullying by a narcissistic leader inhibits productivity and may lead to counterproductive behaviors aimed at undermining the organization's goals. Olive and Cangemi (2015) identified sabotage, theft, and legal action as potential reactions to bullying that hinder the organization's productivity. Authors suggested workers who commit acts of sabotage do so out of frustration over unresolved grievances and perceived mistreatment in the workplace. Such behavior of a narcissistic leader results in reduced productivity and creative output of subordinates. In addition, Olive and Cangemi (2015) also suggested bullying by a narcissistic leader leads to increased employee turnover and gives the organization a reputation as a hostile workplace, thereby hindering future recruiting.

Findings show that the manipulative skills of narcissistic leaders influence how their compensation is set, which may negatively affect companies' finances. Studies have demonstrated that CEOs can increase their pay beyond what is justified by economic determinants through exercising social influence, providing rewards to the board members, and ingratiating themselves with the board (O'Reilly et al., 2014). In addition to their own sense of superiority, narcissists are likely to devalue the contributions of others and overvalue their own contributions (Campbell et al., 2011). Narcissists also have a strong sense of entitlement and a willingness to be aggressive in pursuing what they think is owed to them (Twenge & Campbell, 2009). Therefore, the company is at risk of losing revenue to satisfy the ego of narcissistic leaders. In other words, CEO narcissism may affect the processes and structure of the organization and thus affect feedback and reward systems as well as the organizational structure and workforce composition.

The unpredicted decisions of a narcissistic leader can negatively affect a company externally, which concerns certain areas of companies' operations such as mergers and acquisitions, divestitures, growth strategies, international expansion, product innovation, and brand image. In addition, as narcissistic CEOs have shown a tendency to manipulate financial earnings, other areas of financial reporting may be affected such as financial reporting choices, capital structures, and risk management. In other words, CEO narcissism may affect the processes and design of the organization and thus affect feedback and reward systems as well as the organizational structure and workforce composition.

However, some studies show a positive correlation between a narcissistic leader and a company's financial performance. For example, Chatterjee and Hambrick (2007) found that CEO narcissism positively affects performance extremes, measured as deviations from average industry stock returns or return on assets (ROA) and performance fluctuation (the change in ROA year over year). In addition, Olsen, Dworkis, and Young (2014) found that CEO narcissism positively affects a firm's earnings per share and stock price.

The above findings from these articles show that the narcissistic behavior of a leader impacts the employees' psychological health and job performance. Affected subordinates suffer from stress and depression. It is followed by weak job commitment, burnout and, in some cases, counterproductive behavior. Some of these highly exploited employees have an increased intention to quit. Overall, this indicates that the narcissistic leader has a negative influence on their followers.

Summary

The study's findings present that the main methods to evaluate narcissistic leaders in all organizations are self-reports or others' reports. Various companies use existing narcissism scales and adjust or tailor them to the requirements of a given organization. The importance of this is that a variety of measurement techniques can show there is a correlation between the measurement technique and the perception of a narcissistic leader in an organization.

As mentioned, there is a correlation between the method of leader evaluation and their perception in an organization. In their studies, many researchers have noticed that narcissistic leaders always have a favorable opinion of themselves (Braun, 2017; Foti et al., 2012; Judge, LePine, & Rich, 2006). It was a consequence of the high self-esteem, pride, and egocentrism of narcissists. Narcissists almost always highlight their attributes and contributions to the company's outcomes. However, when subordinates or other employees have a chance to voice their opinion about such a leader, they are more critical in the survey (Campbell et al., 2011; Carlson, Vazire, & Oltmanns, 2011; De Hoogh, Hartog, & Nevicka, 2015; Nevicka et al., 2018). The subordinates are more willing to point out faults and misconduct of narcissistic leaders and their tyrannic and demanding behavior toward the entire work team.

Lastly, the study showed that abusive narcissistic leaders often have a negative influence on employees and coworkers. The main consequence of their abusive supervision is to give employees psychological issues such as stress, depression, a diminished sense of well-being (Hua-Quiang et al., 2018). There was also noticed a significant decrease in job performance and commitment. When this occurs, employees lack job motivation, feel exploited, and express an increased intention to quit (Grijalva et al., 2015; Keller Hansbrough & Jones, 2014). Some researchers have also noticed that the entire organization suffers due to the narcissistic leaders' poor outcomes and unpredicted behavior. This is mainly visible in loss of revenue and of excellent employees.

References

Baars, S. (2015). Narcissistic leadership. https://docplayer.net/56209673-Narcissistic-leadership.html

Babiak, P., & Hare, R. D. (2006). *Snakes in Suits: When Psychopaths Go to Work.* New York: Harper Collins Publishers.

Blair, C., Hoffman, B., & Helland, K. (2008). Narcissism in organizations: A multisource appraisal reflects different perspectives. *Human Performance* 21:254–276. https://link.springer.com/chapter/10.1007/978-3-319-60330-8_4

Boddy, C. R. (2014). Corporate psychopaths, conflict, employee affective well-being and counterproductive work behaviour. *Journal of Business Ethics* 121: 107–121. http://dx.doi.org/10.1007/s10551-013-1688-0

Braun, S. (2017). Leader narcissism and outcomes in organizations: A review at multiple levels of analysis and implications for future research. *Frontiers in Psychology* 8: 773. https://www.frontiersin.org/articles/10.3389/fpsyg.2017.00773/full

Braun, S., Aydin, N., Frey, D., & Peus, C. (2016). Leader narcissism predicts malicious envy and supervisor-targeted counterproductive work behavior – evidence from field and experimental research. *Journal of Business Ethics* 151: 725–741. http://dro.dur.ac.uk/18920/

Campbell, K. W., Hoffman, B. J., Campbell, S. M., & Marchisio, G. (2011). Narcissism in organizational contexts. *Human Resource Management Review* 21: 268–284. https://digitalcommons.kennesaw.edu/facpubs/1582/

Carlson, E., Vazire, S., & Oltmanns, T. (2011). You probably think this paper's about you: Narcissists' perceptions of their personality and reputation. *Journal of Personality and Social Psychology* 101: 185–201. https://www.ncbi.nlm.nih.gov/pmc/articles/PMC3119754/

Chatterjee, A., & Hambrick, D. (2007). It's all about me: Narcissistic chief executive officers and their effects on company strategy and performance. *Administrative Science Quarterly* 52: 351–386. https://journals.sagepub.com/doi/abs/10.2189/asqu.52.3.351

De Hoogh, A., Hartog, D., & Nevicka, B. (2015). Gender differences in the perceived effectiveness of narcissistic leaders. *Applied Psychology* 64: 473–498. https://onlinelibrary.wiley.com/doi/abs/10.1111/apps.12015

Foti, R., Bray, B., Thompson, N., & Allgood, S. (2012). Know thy self, know thy leader: Contributions of a pattern-oriented approach to examining leader perceptions. *The Leadership Quarterly* 23(4): 702–717. https://www.sciencedirect.com/science/article/pii/S1048984312000240

Galvin, B., Lange, D., & Ashforth, B. (2014). Narcissistic organizational identification: Seeing oneself as central to the organization's identity. *Academy of Management Review* 40. https://journals.aom.org/doi/abs/10.5465/amr.2013.0103

Galvin, B. M., Waldman, D., & Balthazard, P. A. (2010). Visionary communication qualities as mediators of the relationship between narcissism and attributions of leader charisma. *Personnel Psychology* 63(3): 509–537. https://doi.org/10.1111/j.1744-6570.2010.01179.x

Grijalva, E., Harms, P., Newman, D., Gaddis, B., & Fraley, R. (2015). Narcissism and leadership: A meta-analytic review of linear and nonlinear relationships. *Personnel Psychology* 68: 1–47. https://onlinelibrary.wiley.com/doi/abs/10.1111/peps.12072

Hart, W., Adams, J., Burton, A., & Tortoriello, G. (2017). Narcissism and self-presentation: Profiling grandiose and vulnerable narcissists' self-presentation tactic use. *Personality and Individual Differences* 104: 48–57. https://www.sciencedirect.com/science/article/abs/pii/S0191886916308121. https://link.springer.com/article/10.1007/s10551-012-1296-4

Hua-Quiang, W., Guang-Lei, Z., Zhi-Hui, D., & Zhi-Hui, C. (2018). How supervisor narcissism contributes to employee silence: Roles of negative anticipations and leader–member exchange. *Social Behavior and Personality* 46(4): 653–666. https://www.sbp-journal.com/index.php/sbp/article/view/6815

Judge, T., LePine, J., & Rich, B. (2006). Loving yourself abundantly: Relationship of the narcissistic personality to self- and other perceptions of workplace deviance, leadership, and task and contextual performance. *Journal of Applied Psychology* 91(4): 762–776. https://asu.pure.elsevier.com/en/publications/loving-yourself-abundantly-relationship-of-the-narcissistic-perso

Keller Hansbrough, T., & Jones, G. (2014). Inside the minds of narcissists: How narcissistic leaders' cognitive processes contribute to abusive supervision.

Zeitschrift für Psychologie 222(4): 214–220. https://econtent.hogrefe.com/doi/10.1027/2151-2604/a000188

Liao, S., Zhou, X., Guo, Z., & Li, Z. (2017). How does leader narcissism influence employee voice: The attribution of leader impression management and leader-member exchange. *International Journal of Environmental Research and Public Health* 16: 1819. https://www.mdpi.com/1660-4601/16/10/1819

Mainah, F., & Perkins, V. (2016). Narcissism in organizational leadership. http://www.docdatabase.net/more-narcissism-in-organizational-leadership-fredah-mainah--1327285.html

Martin, S. R., Cote, S., & Woodruff, T. (2016). Echoes of our upbringing: How growing up wealthy or poor relates to narcissism, leader behavior, and leader effectiveness. *Academy of Management Journal* 59: 2157–2177. https://www.icos.umich.edu/sites/default/files/lecturereadinglists/Martin_et_al.pdf

Maslow, A. (1970). *Motivation and Personality*, Second Edition. New York: Harper and Row.

Nevicka, B., Van Vianen, A., De Hoogh, A., & Voorn, B. (2018). Narcissistic leaders: An asset or a liability? Leader visibility, follower responses, and group-level absenteeism. *Journal of Applied Psychology* 103: 703–723. https://dare.uva.nl/personal/search?identifier=3206d78e-0bdd-43d2-9ba5-98c5d2cd6157

Nevicka, B., Velden, F., Hoogh, A., & Vianen, A. (2011). Reality at odds with perceptions: Narcissistic leaders and group performance. *Psychological Science* 22: 1259–1264. https://journals.sagepub.com/doi/10.1177/0956797611417259

Olive, K., & Cangemi, J. P. (2015). Workplace bullies why they are successful and what can be done about it? *Psychology and Education – An Interdisciplinary Journal.* Western Kentucky University. https://www.researchgate.net/profile/Erez-Zverling/publication/304951451_Betrayal_of_trust_Intimate_partner_bullying_IPB/links/61baded7fd2cbd7200a31e85/Betrayal-of-trust-Intimate-partner-bullying-IPB.pdf#page=45

Olsen, K., Dworkis, K. K., & Young, S. M. (2014). CEO narcissism and accounting: A picture of profits. *Journal of Management Accounting Research* 26(2): 243–267. https://papers.ssrn.com/sol3/papers.cfm?abstract_id=2115067

Ong, C., Roberts, R., Calum, A., Woodman, T., & Akehurst, S. (2016). The leadership is sinking: A temporal investigation of narcissistic leadership. *Journal of Personality* 84: 237–247. https://onlinelibrary.wiley.com/doi/abs/10.1111/jopy.12155

O'Reilly, C., Doerr, B., Caldwell, D., & Chatman, J. (2014). Narcissistic CEOs and executive compensation. *The Leadership Quarterly* 25: 218–231. https://www.sciencedirect.com/science/article/pii/S1048984313000805

Owens, B., Wallace, A., & Waldman, D. (2015). Leader narcissism and follower outcomes: The counterbalancing effect of leader humility. *Journal of Applied Psychology* 100: 1203–1213. https://asu.pure.elsevier.com/en/publications/leader-narcissism-and-follower-outcomes-the-counterbalancing-effe

Paulhus, D. L., & Williams, K. M. (2002). The Dark Triad of personality: Narcissism, Machiavellianism, and psychopathy. *Journal of Research in Personality* 36(6): 556–563. https://academic.microsoft.com/paper/1982777740/citedby/search?q=The%20Dark%20Triad%20of%20personality%3A%20Narcissism%2C%20Machiavellianism%2C%20and%20psychopathy&qe=RId%253D1982777740&f=&orderBy=0

Patel, P., & Cooper, D. (2014). The harder they fall, the faster they rise: Approach and avoidance focus in narcissistic CEOs. *Strategic Management Journal* 35: 1528–1540. https://onlinelibrary.wiley.com/doi/10.1002/smj.2162

Resick, C., Whitman, D., Weingarden, S., & Hiller, N. (2009). The bright-side and the dark-side of CEO personality: Examining core self-evaluations, narcissism, transformational leadership, and strategic influence. *Journal of Applied Psychology* 94(6): 1365–1381. https://www.sciencedirect.com/science/article/pii/S0191886912000530

Rosenthal, S., & Pittinsky, T. (2006). Narcissistic leadership. *The Leadership Quarterly* 17: 617–633. https://www.researchgate.net/profile/Seth_Rosenthal/publication/223046510_Narcissistic_Leadership/links/5d1f5ac192851cf44068903f/Narcissistic-Leadership.pdf

Schilling, J., & Schyns, B. (2015). The causes and consequences of bad leadership. https://doi.org/10.1027/2151-2604/a000185

Sedikides, C., & Campbell, K. (2017). Narcissistic force meets systemic resistance: The Energy Clash Model. *Perspectives on Psychological Science* 12: 400–421. https://eprints.soton.ac.uk/404441/1/__filestore.soton.ac.uk_users_gg_mydocuments_constantine%2520publications%2520pdf%2527s_In%2520Press_Sedikides%2520%2520Campbell_in%2520press%2520Perspectives%2520on%2520Psychological%2520Science.pdf

Seigner, E., Coyne, I., Randall, P., & Parker, J. (2007). Personality traits of bullies as a contributory factor in workplace bullying: An exploratory study. *International Journal of Organization Theory & Behavior* 10(1): 118–132.

Sosik, J. J., Chun, J. U., & Zhu, W. (2014). Hang on to your ego: The moderating role of leader narcissism on relationships between leader charisma and follower psychological empowerment and moral identity. *Journal of Business Ethics* 120: 65–80. https://doi.org/10.1007/s10551-013-1651-0

Tokarev, A., Phillips, A., Hughes, D., & Irwing, P. (2017). Leader dark traits, workplace bullying, and employee depression: Exploring mediation and the role of the dark core. *Journal of Abnormal Psychology* 126: 911–920. https://psycnet.apa.org/record/2017-49368-007

Twenge, J. M., & Campbell, W. K. (2009). *The Narcissism Epidemic: Living in the Age of Entitlement.* New York: Simon & Schuster.

Zhu, D. H., & Chen, G. (2015). CEO narcissism and the impact of prior board experience on corporate strategy. *Administrative Science Quarterly* 60(1): 31–65. https://doi.org/10.1177/0001839214554989

5 Narcissistic Leadership and the Impact on the Leader-Follower Relationship

In recent decades, society has witnessed an increase of individuals with narcissistic personality traits, and these individuals often hold a leadership position in various organizations. The existing research presents only general information on this topic, hence the need to investigate it carefully. I have examined different methods to evaluate a narcissistic leader in organizations to test if there is a correlation between the evaluation method and how the narcissistic leader is perceived. Therefore, this study's primary question is how the different types of independent variables, such as self-ratings and other-ratings of narcissistic leaders, determine how narcissistic leaders are perceived in an organization. The second issue examined is the impact that the opinion of a narcissistic leader has on employees' emotional health, job commitment, performance, and company effectiveness.

The presented research has conducted an article review of already existing data on the subject of narcissism, narcissistic personality traits, narcissistic leaders, the perception of a narcissist, and methods of evaluation of narcissistic leaders in the organization. This form of study method is the most appropriate method for the proposed topic because many researchers have already examined similar issues. Therefore, there is a variety of data available on this subject. The research extends the problem to show that the perception of leaders is linked with their evaluation, which negatively affects other employees, especially lower-level ones. Through this research method, this study has also found that such leaders' narcissistic behavior negatively influences employees of a given organization, causing mental problems such as stress and depression, lack of job motivation, lower effectiveness and job satisfaction, and in some cases, resignation from work.

Findings

The presented information is built upon the performed research. It presents an overview of the findings on the positive and negative perception of a narcissistic leader in an organization. It also discusses the positive and negative outcomes of such a leader on their followers. The next step is

DOI: 10.4324/9781003260646-5

to present the need for further research on the topic of the perception of a narcissistic leader in organizations and how this affects their followers' personality traits.

Perception of Narcissistic Leader vs. Method of Evaluation

The research shows that organizations use various forms for leader assessment – the ones focused on in this study are self-ratings and others' ratings. As demonstrated throughout the study, one variable appears to influence how a narcissistic leader is perceived, and that is the method of leader evaluation. The findings show that companies mostly use the Narcissistic Personality Inventory (NPI; Galvin, Waldman, & Balthazard, 2010; Nevicka et al., 2011; Ong et al., 2016), the NPI-16 (De Hoogh, Hartog, & Nevicka, 2015; Foti et al., 2012; Nevicka et al., 2011; Owens et al., 2015) or the CPI (Blair, Hoffman, & Helland, 2008) to assess the level of narcissism in an individual. Nevertheless, it has been noticed that the results of such an evaluation highly depend on the participants of the survey. The surveys are usually distributed to leaders (whether they are managers, supervisors, or CEOs) and their followers and subordinates.

The study results demonstrate that the dyadic level of analysis depends on the method of narcissistic leader evaluation. The evidence shows that when others assessed their narcissistic leader, the leader was perceived negatively. However, other variables, such as time or leader-follower relationships, also influence the opinion of the narcissistic leader (Galvin, Waldman, & Balthazard, 2010). The findings' analysis presents a slight inconsistency in the results, which occurs when the assessment is performed by close friends or family of the narcissistic leader (Baars, 2015). It is a result of the close relationship that the narcissists have with their friends and families; they manipulate these people to protect their good image. Whether due to fear or the need to protect their image, those closely related to the narcissistic leader have a favorable opinion of them.

The other inconsistency is related to the time of the narcissistic leader's evaluation. The evidence shows that, if these leaders are assessed at the beginning of their career, they are more favorably perceived. This phenomenon is called leader emergence (Grijalva et al., 2014; Schyns & Schilling 2015) or leaders' first impression activity (Carlson, Vazire, & Oltmanns, 2011). In turn, the longer the followers interact or are under their narcissistic leader's supervision, the less favorable feedback they have about them. This correlates with the personality traits of narcissists; thus, such individuals tend to present all their best features to create a good impression to later strive on it as a leader. Furthermore, over time the effectiveness of a narcissist decreases, and as follows, his ratings of good leaders drop as well.

It has been noticed across various levels of analysis that self-reports almost always show that a narcissistic leader has a positive perception of themselves. This is because narcissists speak of themselves highly (Hart et al., 2017) and see themselves as ideal leaders (Foti et al., 2012). The findings indicate that a narcissistic leader's self-rating is biased because they are based on a one-sided opinion of the narcissistic individual. The suggestion is to omit this form of evaluation when examining a narcissistic leader' perception by his followers.

The Outcome of a Narcissistic Leader

The research also measured the influence that a narcissistic leader has on the outcomes of their followers and the entire organization. By examining the followers' perceptions of narcissistic leaders, the study found that the leaders' dominant personality traits determined how leaders affect their followers.

A person with narcissistic personality traits is predisposed to achieve success in their professional life as a leader. They are a great asset to organizations due to the positive characteristics of their personality. They are positively perceived in their interviews; therefore, they are more often chosen as leaders at all levels of an organization. The literature review supports this and terms this phenomenon narcissistic leader emergence (Nevicka et al., 2011). Narcissistic leaders are also skilled at radiating an image of a prototypically effective leader with bold vision and charisma (Galvin, Waldman, & Balthazard, 2010). This is why so many narcissists are chosen as world leaders or CEOs of big organizations. As the research findings show, narcissistic leaders are valued for their risk-taking in pursuing new internalization investments and new technology. They are known to have fantastic ideas and strategies, and companies profit from such individuals' knowledge. However, the charisma and charm presented by narcissists do not determine how their followers will perceive them.

Narcissism is an essential addition to the list of characteristics that make leaders more predisposed to abusive behavior. The study results demonstrate that there are negative ramifications of this behavior on the followers' daily functioning at work, including psychological distress and lowered work performance, as found in the literature review. Followers who worked for a leader with highly narcissistic traits perceived their leader as more abusive, which led to poor work completion (Owens et al. 2015). Job satisfaction drops due to burnout, which results in lowered performance and increased intention to quit (Keller Hansbrough & Jones, 2014).

The research findings correspond with the literature review outcomes, which show that leaders' abusive behavior or bullying results in significant psychological distress of their followers. Such followers experience emotional exhaustion, stress, and depression (Hua-Qiang, Guang-Lei, & Zhi-Hui, 2018; Tokarev et al., 2017). Through the waves of excitement, narcissistic leaders create instability in the office and among their subordinates (Nevicka et al., 2018), which also deflates the trust that people place in the leader and affecting the subordinates' sense of psychological safety. The employees' self-esteem drops, thus also lowering their prosocial behavior (Liu et al., 2017). Some employees may even feel envious and may want to seek revenge while interacting with highly abusive leaders. The research findings also show that certain personality traits, such as low self-esteem, make followers particularly vulnerable to leader abuse (Nevicka et al., 2018). It is suggested to perform further study to deepen the topic with inclusion of followers' personality traits and correlating these with the perception of the narcissistic leader.

The literature review has a few limitations. At first, while performing the study, a specific set of articles were selected, which were peer-reviewed scholarly articles retrieved from the online library of California Southern University. At the same time, those criteria excluded some articles that could be of great value for the research. The choice of articles demonstrates the study's empirical rigor; however, the criteria may be biased and valuable information could have been omitted. The study was conducted using articles that included only two assessment methods of narcissistic leaders: self-ratings and others' ratings. However, this also limited the number of reviewed articles and eliminated other study designs such as computer simulations, case studies, field surveys, and laboratory experiments.

Secondly, the study only measures narcissism among leaders, disregarding two other dark traits: Machiavellianism and psychopathy (Jones & Paulhus, 2014). Throughout the research, it was also impossible to control and isolate the unique effects of narcissism. This analysis also generalized for all followers. It excluded the impact of their personality traits on the perception of a narcissistic leader in the workplace. The study also neglected to measure a narcissistic leader's opinion on the team level, namely the personal connection between the narcissistic leader and their coworkers.

Implications for Professional Practice

The main focus of this study is to show that the narcissistic leader evaluation methods influence how such a leader is perceived in an organization. The results of the research proved that there is a correlation between the two variables. However, it also indicates that other factors, taken under consideration, can slightly modify the study results. The results of the research demonstrate that social studies will profit benefit from these findings.

The literature on the topic of narcissistic leaders shows that narcissists are highly desired as leaders in organizations. They possess several features in common with the traits of successful people. Such individuals are optimistic, socially skilled, and perform well in public and in challenging situations. They are also confident, have a grand vision, are not afraid of taking risks, and are persistent in pursuing their goals (Keller Hansbrough & Jones, 2014; Owens et al., 2015). One may think that such an individual is the best leader possible. However, the research shows that although narcissistic leaders can be of great value to the organization, they may adversely affect their employees and subordinates. This study adds to the existing research. It indicates that a narcissistic leader's perception varies depending on the person evaluating the leader's job.

The research empirically proved that a narcissistic leader's perception is linked with the methods of leader evaluation. Through the literature review, I presented that a narcissistic leader is perceived positively or negatively. Others' ratings, which are the ratings given by followers and employees of a narcissistic leader, often demonstrate that others have an unfavorable opinion of a narcissistic leader. The research adds to the current study that those subordinates who had an unfavorable opinion of their leader described them as arrogant, manipulative (Nevicka et al., 2013), self-centered, unethical (Hua-Qiang, Guang-Lei, & Zhi-Hui, 2018), abusive, credit taking (Keller Hansbrough & Jones, 2014), cruel, and entitled to everything (Galvin, Waldman, & Balthazard, 2010). This information indicates that narcissists' followers often do not find any positive features of their managers and mostly use negative adjectives to describe them. Thus, this study's insight is that when evaluating a narcissistic leader, organizations should gather the assessments of the leaders' followers as this will give them more accurate results and allow them to gather an honest opinion.

The study also demonstrates that narcissistic leaders can be perceived in a positive light. This occurs when the evaluation of such a leader is performed by the leader through the self-rating assessment. In this instance, such individuals ascribes to themselves features such as being a risk takers (Owens et al., 2015), charismatic, visionary (Galvin, Waldman, & Balthazard, 2010), dynamic, and confident (Nevicka et al., 2013). These features are highly desirable in leaders; therefore, many narcissists are chosen for high-level positions in organizations. At this time, narcissists express self-serving bias, which is ascribed as a tendency to attribute positive events to one's character (Cayirdag, 2020). However, the study also found that when narcissists perform self-evaluation, they omit the less desirable features of their character that may make them be perceived in a negative light. This information benefits the social study because it implies that narcissists fail to see anything wrong in their behavior toward their followers or ignore their wrongdoings to ensure they have a favorable review. They are also keen on manipulating the assessment to their favor; therefore, self-ratings are biased and provide false information.

The research also discovered that other variables could influence the change in perception of a narcissistic leader in an organization. One of the variables that could impact the results is leadership emergence versus leadership effectiveness. The study implies that a narcissistic leader expresses great leadership emergence, which results in a positive perception of such a leader among their followers (Ong et al., 2016). This is related to the narcissist's ability to display authority, confidence, and convince followers of their grand vision (Keller Hansbrough & Jones, 2014). Their charm, excellent communication skills, and readiness to change the world make people think highly of such an individual; therefore, the evaluation of such a leader at the beginning of their work at the organization may vary (Carlson, Vazire, & Oltmanns, 2011). The research also shows that the longer the narcissistic leader guides their employees, the less favorable the employees' opinion is of them. Such an occurrence is worth considering while performing further study in this matter.

As expressed through the research some leader evaluations can be biased because they are completed by the leader's close acquaintances. This is an example of confirmation bias conducted by people closely related to narcissistic leaders. It involves favoring information that confirms their previously existing beliefs on those leaders (Heshmat, 2015). Confirmation bias relies on views once formed by family and friends about that narcissist (possibly during leadership emergence) and supported by bits of data that make these people feel good about their narcissistic leader. This is a valuable insight into the current study on narcissistic leaders in organizations. It implies that leader assessment results may be manipulated by assigning significant others or close friends as assesses (Baars, 2015). The suggestion is to eliminate any people with a close relationship with the narcissistic leader. This will ensure that honest responses will be inputted and that one can get an honest idea of the perception of such an individual in the organization.

Lastly, throughout the study, it has been noted that leader narcissism has an inhibitory effect on employee behavior and well-being at work. The current research has analyzed abusive behavior or supervision in the workplace. The present study extends the outcomes of narcissistic leadership in the previous research by grouping it into two main categories: an employee's psychological and physical dysfunction. The psychological distress includes lower self-esteem and increased levels of stress and depression (Hua-Qiang, Guang-Lei, & Zhi-Hui, 2018; Judge et al., 2015; Keller Hansbrough & Jones, 2014; Mainah & Perkins, 2016). Physical distress is associated with lower prosocial behavior (Liu et al., 2017), lower job performance and commitment, and higher burnout (Nevicka et al., 2018).

The study points out a need to strengthen the awareness of the narcissistic individual because these behaviors profoundly impact employees who are subject to narcissistic leadership.

Recommendations for Research

The research's main strength lies in the replicability of the findings across the chosen samples and its presentation of a more detailed study on the matter. The presented literature review focuses on the perception of a narcissistic leader as correlated with the narcissistic leader's evaluation methods, namely self-ratings and others' ratings. Although the study gives insights into how the narcissist is perceived, it omits discussing other employees working at various organizational levels.

First, there is a strong suggestion to convey future studies based on current findings with the inclusion of the narcissistic leader's peer-to-peer perception. The present research mainly shows the relation between the leader and their subordinates, which may indicate that the fear of their leader's abusive supervision may distort followers' opinions of their leader (Owens et al., 2015). Employees may be afraid to speak up about their leader's abusive behavior; these leaders are higher up in the organization and thus employees may worry that, their narcissistic leaders have higher ranks in the organization, and therefore the subordinates voices may not be heard. The peer-to-peer assessment should include the narcissist's relationship with other leaders working at the same organizational level. Such a study can give an insight into how non-narcissistic colleagues working at the same level as the narcissist perceive the narcissist. This would thus eliminate all limitations related to the narcissistic leader's various functions and followers. Further research could also be extended to analyzing the interaction between narcissistic CEOs and their management teams. This could surface information on whether managers perceive their narcissistic CEOs more favorably than followers perceive their narcissistic manager.

Second, I advocate to perform research to include different subfactors of narcissism and examine the two dark traits, namely Machiavellianism and psychopathy. The current literature review had limited the findings to narcissistic leaders without verifying the other more adverse traits of such a personality (Nevicka et al., 2011). Those with these two dark characteristics are known to be more abusive toward their followers, due to their vivid personality characteristics, which are the overlap between narcissism and psychopathy and are called the 'dark core' (Tokarev et al., 2017). It would be interesting to measure if psychopathy or Machiavellianism has a more significant impact on the followers' perception of their leader. This research would also present information on whether such leaders' negative opinions are related to more chances for workplace bullying and abuse toward their subordinates (Tokarev et al., 2017).

Third, I recommend further research on the perception of narcissistic leaders in the organization to account for the followers' personality traits. The current literature has focused on the personality characteristic of narcissistic leaders, making them a crucial aspect of the negative assessment of such a leader. However, the followers' personality traits may also indicate that some individuals are more prone to abuse and workplace bullying than others. Although some researchers have measured the correlation between the followers' low self-esteem and leader narcissism, many other personality characteristics may influence whether a person is susceptible to the negative treatment of a narcissistic leader (Nevicka et al., 2018). Future research should also incorporate followers' socioemotional and human-capital characteristics to measure their perceptions of the narcissistic leaders. Such research may deepen the current study by using new data on followers and determining whether some are more predisposed to leaders' abusive behavior than others.

Lastly, it is recommended to extend the current research by implementing a given organization's organizational culture, including procedures and activities undertaken to improve teamwork or fight abusive behavior. Incorporating those variables may influence the perception of narcissistic leaders from bad to worse, depending on whether these factors promote prosocial behavior. Recent research suggests that leadership narcissism deteriorates over time; therefore, it is strongly recommended to include variables such as how long the leader has been employed in the organization (Grijalva et al., 2014). Furthermore, the current findings may be examined by including the narcissist's relationship with their followers. It has been mentioned earlier that the close acquaintance between a leader and his followers (family relations or friendship) may deteriorate the study; thus, such followers will always give positive feedback (Baars, 2015). Hence, future research should account for these possibilities. The final fruitful direction for future research should build upon current findings utilizing multisource data (e.g., independent ratings of followers' and narcissists' personality traits) that is objective (including all possible forms of leader evaluation) and collected longitudinally.

Conclusions

Society is becoming more self-centered and egocentric. Many people want to be the center of attention, be admired by others, and be at the top of their careers. These people also have skills that are highly desirable for leadership positions in many organizations. Those and many other features, when ascribed to individuals, make these individuals narcissists. Narcissistic personality and narcissists have recently been of interest to scholars. Attention has been paid to the negative impact that a narcissist can have on the people surrounding them, especially in an organizational setting. This research has shown how the narcissistic leader is perceived by their subordinates and the impact of this on their employees. I hope that this research will help psychology and encourage researchers to extend the research on the topic of corporate narcissism or leadership narcissism.

References

Baars, S. (2015). Narcissistic leadership. https://docplayer.net/56209673-Narcissistic-leadership.html

Blair, C., Hoffman, B., & Helland, K. (2008). Narcissism in organizations: A multisource appraisal reflects different perspectives. *Human Performance* 21: 254–276. https://link.springer.com/chapter/10.1007/978-3-319-60330-8_4

Carlson, E., Vazire, S., & Oltmanns, T. (2011). You probably think this paper's about you: Narcissists' perceptions of their personality and reputation. *Journal of Personality and Social Psychology* 101: 185–201. https://www.ncbi.nlm.nih.gov/pmc/articles/PMC3119754/

Cayirdag, N. (2020). *Attribution. Encyclopedia of Creativity* (Third Edition). https://www.sciencedirect.com/science/article/pii/B9780128093245218907

De Hoogh, A., Hartog, D., & Nevicka, B. (2015). Gender differences in the perceived effectiveness of narcissistic leaders. *Applied Psychology* 64: 473–498. https://onlinelibrary.wiley.com/doi/abs/10.1111/apps.12015

Foti, R., Bray, B., Thompson, N., & Allgood, S. (2012). Know thy self, know thy leader: Contributions of a pattern-oriented approach to examining leader perceptions. *The Leadership Quarterly* 23(4): 702–717. https://www.sciencedirect.com/science/article/pii/S1048984312000240

Galvin, B. M., Waldman, D., & Balthazard, P. A. (2010). Visionary communication qualities as mediators of the relationship between narcissism and attributions of leader charisma. *Personnel Psychology* 63(3): 509–537. https://doi.org/10.1111/j.1744-6570.2010.01179.x

Grijalva, E., Harms, P., Newman, D., Gaddis, B., & Fraley, R. (2014). Narcissism and leadership: A meta-analytic review of linear and nonlinear relationships. *Personnel Psychology* 68: 1–47. https://onlinelibrary.wiley.com/doi/abs/10.1111/peps.12072

Hart, W., Adams, J., Burton, A., & Tortoriello, G. (2017). Narcissism and self-presentation: Profiling grandiose and vulnerable narcissists' self-presentation tactic use. *Personality and Individual Differences* 104: 48–57. https://www.sciencedirect.com/science/article/abs/pii/S0191886916308121. https://link.springer.com/article/10.1007/s10551-012-1296-4

Heshmat, S. (2015, April 23). What is confirmation bias? https://www.psychologytoday.com/us/blog/science-choice/201504/what-is-confirmation-bias

Hua-Qiang, W., Guang-Lei, Z., Zhi-Hui, D., & Zhi-Hui, C. (2018). How supervisor narcissism contributes to employee silence: Roles of negative anticipations and leader–member exchange. *Social Behavior and Personality* 46(4): 653–666. https://www.sbp-journal.com/index.php/sbp/article/view/6815

Jones, D., & Paulhus, D. (2014). Introducing the Short Dark Triad (SD3): A brief measure of dark personality traits. *Assessment* 21: 28–41. https://journals.sagepub.com/doi/10.1177/1073191113514105

Judge, T., LePine, J., & Rich, B. (2015). Loving yourself abundantly: Relationship of the narcissistic personality to self- and other perceptions of workplace deviance, leadership, and task and contextual performance. *Journal of Applied Psychology* 91(4): 762–776. https://asu.pure.elsevier.com/en/publications/loving-yourself-abundantly-relationship-of-the-narcissistic-perso

Keller Hansbrough, T., & Jones, G. (2014). Inside the minds of narcissists: How narcissistic leaders' cognitive processes contribute to abusive supervision. *Zeitschrift für Psychologie* 222(4): 214–220. https://econtent.hogrefe.com/doi/10.1027/2151-2604/a000188

Liu, H., Chiang, J., Fehr, R., Xu, M., & Wang, S. (2017). How do leaders react when treated unfairly? Leader narcissism and self-interested behavior in response to unfair treatment. *Journal of Applied Psychology* 102(11): 1590–1599. https://insights.ovid.com/applied-psychology/japsy/2017/11/000/leaders-react-when-treated-unfairly-leader/6/00004565

Mainah, F., & Perkins, V. (2016). Narcissism in organizational leadership. http://www.docdatabase.net/more-narcissism-in-organizational-leadership-fredah-mainah--1327285.html

Nevicka, B., De Hoogh, A. H., Van Vianen, A. E., & Ten Velden, F. S. (2013). Uncertainty enhances the preference for narcissistic leaders. *European Journal of Social Psychology* 43: 370–380. https://www.narcis.nl/publication/RecordID/oai%3Adare.uva.nl%3Apublications%2F84d8e93b-f2a0-41f4-9475-20a793aeb194

Nevicka, B., Van Vianen, A., De Hoogh, A., & Voorn, B. (2018). Narcissistic leaders: An asset or a liability? Leader visibility, follower responses, and group-level absenteeism. *Journal of Applied Psychology* 103: 703–723. https://dare.uva.nl/personal/search?identifier=3206d78e-0bdd-43d2-9ba5-98c5d2cd6157

Nevicka, B., Velden, F., Hoogh, A., & Vianen, A. (2011). Reality at odds with perceptions: Narcissistic leaders and group performance. *Psychological Science* 22: 1259–1264. https://journals.sagepub.com/doi/10.1177/0956797611417259

Ong, C., Roberts, R., Calum, A., Woodman, T., & Akehurst, S. (2016). The leadership is sinking: A temporal investigation of narcissistic leadership. *Journal of Personality* 84: 237–247. https://onlinelibrary.wiley.com/doi/abs/10.1111/jopy.12155

Owens, B., Wallace, A., & Waldman, D. (2015). Leader narcissism and follower outcomes: The counterbalancing effect of leader humility. *Journal of Applied Psychology* 100: 1203–1213. https://asu.pure.elsevier.com/en/publications/leader-narcissism-and-follower-outcomes-the-counterbalancing-effe

Schyns, B., & Schilling, J. (2015). The causes and consequences of bad leadership. *Zeitschrift für Psychologie* 222(4): 187–189. https://doi.org/10.1027/2151-2604/a000185

Tokarev, A., Phillips, A., Hughes, D., & Irwing, P. (2017). Leader dark traits, workplace bullying, and employee depression: Exploring mediation and the role of the dark core. *Journal of Abnormal Psychology* 126: 911–920. https://psycnet.apa.org/record/2017-49368-007

Index